AMERICAN

SERIES EDITOR, EDWARD FOLEY

Lay Preaching

State of the Question

PATRICIA A. PARACHINI, S.N.J.M.

A Liturgical Press Book

 THE LITURGICAL PRESS
Collegeville, Minnesota

1   2   3   4   5   6   7   8   9

Library of Congress Cataloging-in-Publication Data

Parachini, Patricia A., 1940–
    Lay preaching : state of the question / Patricia A. Parachini.
       p.   cm. — (American essays in liturgy)
    Includes bibliographical references.
    ISBN 0-8146-2549-5 (alk. paper)
    1. Lay preaching.   2. Catholic preaching.   I. Title.   II. Series:
American essays in liturgy (Collegeville, Minn.)
BV4235.L3P37   1999
251—dc21   98-24490
                                                   CIP

Contents

Introduction

Most Christians, especially Roman Catholics, would not consider themselves preachers, and yet, by the call we share through our baptism each of us is mandated to preach—to proclaim the "good news" to all we meet.

Although the content of preaching has been variously described and defined, at the heart of its meaning is the good news that God has sent the beloved one, Jesus. That same God has raised Jesus to new life, giving us the assurance that we, too, will be raised to new life here and now and will experience the fullness of that life when God's reign comes at the end-time. The Christian call to preach is a call to proclaim with conviction this gospel, which offers all of humankind new possibilities for life and grace.

Proclaiming the gospel (preaching) is effected in many ways throughout our lives as Christian believers, especially in words and works of reconciliation, healing, and justice. We preach through the witness of our life, through teaching, through ordinary conversation and personal testimony to God's love, as well as through a more formal proclamation in worship. Preaching is the call of all the baptized.

It is helpful for our discussion to keep in mind that "preaching," as generally understood and most frequently used, is not primarily a written activity but oral, and it is in this way that we will use the term throughout this volume. It is a *speech-act*[1]—a form of public discourse. This oral activity of preaching is a broad category, or *genus,* which includes a number of different types or *species,* for example, pre-evangelistic preaching, evangelization, catechetical preaching or catechesis, preaching in church, and liturgical preaching (the preaching of the homily *per se*).[2] Our references to lay preaching include all of these types of preaching.

Throughout this book, "lay preaching" will be understood as any form of preaching rendered by a baptized Christian who has not been ordained a deacon, priest, or bishop. These lay preachers include also members of religious congregations, orders, or societies of women and men who are not ordained. Although they are in some sense neither "lay" nor "cleric," members of these religious congregations, orders, or societies who are not ordained are considered to be laity in those canons that refer to lay preaching in the 1983 revised Code of Canon Law.[3]

For Roman Catholics, attention to the question of lay preaching was minimal immediately after Vatican II but has been a growing issue of concern since the mid-1980s. The reality of lay preaching is no longer something in the distant future but is a present and growing phenomenon. One need only observe the increasing numbers of lay parish directors who are presiding and preaching at Communion services or services of the word throughout the United States.[4] In addition, since the promulgation of the revised Code of Canon Law, increasing numbers of books and articles have treated the topic in depth and have surfaced significant questions.[5] It seems both timely and urgent that this issue be addressed in a systematic way if the needs of God's people for hearing the word are to be met.

Documents from Vatican II up to the present have placed a new emphasis on the important role of the laity in sharing responsibility for the spread of the gospel (e.g., *Apostolicam actuositatem* 6; *Evangelii nuntiandi* 70). The 1983 revised Code of Canon Law, too, acknowledges the call of all the baptized to take an active role in the proclamation of the gospel: ". . . they can also be called upon to cooperate with the bishop and presbyters in the exercise of the ministry of the word."[6] The practice of lay preaching has been reintroduced and is developing into a common practice in many parts of the country. It seems that the time is ripe for further exploration.

In this volume we intend to focus our attention primarily on one type of lay preaching, that is, liturgical preaching, since that seems to be a highly problematic area and the one most frequently discussed and debated. It is the only type of preaching listed above from which laity are regularly excluded, although exceptions are allowed and have been made. However, since the distinctions among the different types of preaching is a relatively new phenomenon, much of the discussion in chapter 1 addressing the history of lay preaching will deal with lay preaching in general.

In the past ten years throughout the United States there has been a growing interest in the ministry of liturgical preaching among many Roman Catholic women and men who minister in the Church but who are not ordained to the diaconate, priesthood, or episcopacy. Among the variety of circumstances that have precipitated this phenomenon the following seem to be the most influential:

—a significant number of laity have had the opportunity for continuing education in Scripture, theology, liturgical studies, and spirituality;

—more laity have been presiding in liturgical services in their local communities of worship;

—laypersons have been invited to greater involvement in renewed ministries of evangelization and retreat work;

—certain gatherings by their very nature seem to call for preaching by a member of the group itself (e.g., religious orders of women or men with no ordained members);

—in many instances where laypersons have been preaching, the call to lay preaching has been encouraged and affirmed by their local communities of faith.

It is important, then, to pay attention to this growing interest and to assess the needs of the People of God in our time so that we will use our gifts wisely for proclaiming the gospel.

The plan of this work will be, first of all, to highlight significant moments in the history of lay preaching; then we will address some of the major theological and liturgical concerns that are key to a discussion on preaching. We will then examine the pertinent canons on preaching from the 1983 revised Code of Canon Law. Finally, we will describe present practices throughout the United States regarding lay preaching and will raise some of the more fundamental questions to give us a direction for the future.

Since our emphasis is on liturgical preaching in Roman Catholic practice in the United States, we will limit our treatment to Roman Catholic developments and concerns in the discussion of the twentieth century. The questions raised about Church law and the homily are specific to the experience of those in the Roman Catholic communion. But beyond this, since lay preaching appears to be a growing practice in some of the other Christian churches as well, it could be beneficial for Roman Catholics to engage with these others to share experiences and to explore the questions together in order to further the discussion.

Uppermost in our mind as we address these issues and concerns is the awareness that the People of God need to hear the word preached to them well and effectively. This concern that God's people hear the word of God preached effectively "in season and out of season" is the appropriate starting point for any examination of the ministry of preaching, particularly when addressing the question of lay preaching.[7]

1 A Historical Survey

In addressing the issue of preaching in the medieval period, John O'Malley advises us to recognize how complex is the task of understanding the preaching phenomenon in its development through history. Because preaching is an oral medium, *a speech-act*, it cannot be fully captured solely from examining the static written evidence available. By its very nature it is fleeting and difficult to pinpoint. Therefore, to understand it interpreters must take into account such features as the listeners, the setting, the different types of sermon forms, the political, ecclesiastical, and cultural pressures influencing the preacher—all those factors that played a part in forming the preaching event in each historical era.

O'Malley speaks of the trend in the past few decades of examining the preaching phenomenon from its many-faceted influences and components, drawing from the findings of Scripture studies, liturgy, theology, social and cultural history, and other disciplines. It is no longer sufficient to examine preaching as a handmaid to the history of dogma or theology, as was the practice in the past.[8] In his opinion, it is much more evident now that "the history of preaching is not an undifferentiated *continuum,* nor is it the rise and fall of 'true doctrine.' In its various expressions, preaching is part and parcel of general culture, and we understand it best by studying it that way."[9] This is certainly true when we look at the phenomenon of lay preaching throughout the history of the Christian Church.

As the history of preaching attests, lay preaching was a phenomenon that was practiced and accepted for a brief period in the early Church. Then from the fifth century until the Middle Ages it was no longer officially sanctioned. In the Middle Ages lay preaching was reintroduced, even, at times, by ecclesiastical authorities, particularly during the twelfth century. With the Fourth Lateran Council (1215) preaching became once again a clerical preserve. By the time of the Council of Trent (1545–63) the right and responsibility for preaching were explicitly connected with clerical office in the Roman Catholic Church, and lay preaching was formally prohibited. However, with the promulgation of the 1983 revised Code of Canon Law, the doors for the possibility of lay preaching have been opened once again. It is appropriate, therefore, that the topic of lay preaching is the focus of serious discussion among Roman Catholics at the present time. This brief survey will highlight the major moments in the history of lay preaching, thus serving as a catalyst for continued reflection and exploration.

The Christian Scriptures

In her recent book on the theology of preaching, Mary Catherine Hilkert gives more than adequate evidence from the Christian Scriptures that women as well as men not only proclaimed the good news of Jesus' resurrection to the disciples (e.g., John 20:18) but also preached publicly in worship in the early Christian community. In addition, she points out that women, such as Prisca (or Priscilla), along with her husband, Aquila (Acts 18:26), also participated in the teaching ministry, which was closely connected with that of preaching in the early Church and often spoken of synonymously.[10] The exercise of the preaching ministry during this period of the early Christian community appears to be based on the charism for doing it well and effectively and, at least on the surface, does not appear to be dependent upon one's gender or office in the Church.

Nevertheless, as Hilkert notes, two of the passages that have been used to prohibit women from preaching publicly in Christian worship are also part of the canon of the Christian Scriptures, 1 Cor 14:33b-35 and 1 Tim 2:11-15. Obviously lay preaching, especially preaching by women, was a controversial practice right from the beginning.

Hilkert's interpretation of these two passages is helpful in assessing the situation. Her reading of the passage from Corinthians that speaks of women keeping silent in the assembly supports the contention that this passage has been greatly misused. For example, she notes that elsewhere in the same letter Paul refers to women praying and prophesying publicly and does not criticize that practice. Also, she points out that the verb "to speak" (λαλειν) in this passage does not refer to the official functions of preaching or teaching. The second passage from 1 Timothy is a later development and appears to be in conflict with earlier evidence from the Pauline corpus, which mentions the practice of women prophesying and praying in public.

After developing her conclusions based on an examination of the scriptural evidence Hilkert cautions that we cannot ignore the fact that although "the patriarchal bias of the texts may seem evident in an age of critical biblical scholarship, . . . those texts, taken as authoritative and inspired, functioned to prohibit women from preaching in the majority of the Christian churches well into the twentieth century."[11]

Sandra Schneiders' examination of the same two passages raises similar concerns about the conclusions reached. She looks at 1 Corinthians 11, which speaks of Paul's insistence on women wearing a head covering when they pray and prophesy, and notes that this passage establishes the context for 1 Cor 14:33b-35, which is the passage under discussion. Her conclusion is that "this reference seems to indicate rather clearly that women not only spoke in the liturgical assembly but, since prophets, as we know from other early texts such as the *Didache,* offered the Eucharistic prayer and gave what we today call the sermon or homily, women prophets might well have filled these roles."[12] In examining the passage from 1 Timothy, she concludes that "the real reason for the prohibition was ecclesiastical expediency—the felt need to keep the Christian community from appearing socially deviant in a potentially repressive cultural and religious situation."[13]

Concluding her study of these two passages, Schneiders says, ". . . we must say that in all probability women did pray and prophesy, that is, they did the equivalent of preaching in the liturgical assemblies of some of the earliest churches, and Paul, at least, approved of it. Somewhat later, for understandable reasons of expediency, this freedom of women was retrenched in some churches and eventually in all of them."[14]

The Early Church

The threefold Church order of bishop, presbyter, and deacon had developed and was accepted as normative by the end of the second century. At this time the bishop was given the prerogative of preaching or delegating someone else to do so. Hilkert notes that there is some evidence of women presiding and preaching in the Montanist sect of the second century, but by the third century women were explicitly excluded from preaching and teaching in "orthodox" communities, as is indicated in the *Didascalia apostolorum*.

In the third century, Origen (+254?), a layman, was invited by the bishops of Jerusalem and Caesarea to preach. While the prohibition against women preaching continued, the *Apostolic Constitutions* of the fourth century confirmed that with proper training lay*men* could be teachers (and preachers). Hilkert points out that after this no evidence of officially authorized lay preaching is available until the Middle Ages.[15]

Leo the Great

In July 453 Pope Leo the Great (+461) wrote a letter to Bishop Maximus expressing in strong words what had, in fact, by this time become the accepted practice regarding lay preaching: it was no longer permitted:

> Apart from those who are priests of the Lord, no one may dare to claim for himself the right to teach and preach, whether he be monk or layman, one who boasts a reputation for some learning. For, although it is desirable that all the Church's sons be learned in what is right and holy, no one outside the priestly order is to be allowed to assume for himself the rank of preacher. For it is necessary that all things be in order in God's Church; that is, in the one body of Christ, the superior members are to carry out their office, and the inferior members are not to resist the superior ones.[16]

James Coriden points out that the thrust of this letter was later repeated in a variety of forms by popes in the thirteenth and fifteenth centuries. Its content became the basis for the 1917 Code of Canon Law's prohibition of lay preaching.[17]

William Skudlarek raises an interesting point about this letter's prohibition of lay preaching. He says that at that period of history it was emphasized that preachers be both "learned" and licensed (from a bishop) to preach. Since in this letter Leo is objecting to a monk or layman arrogating to himself the right to preach, Skudlarek believes that the letter "would seem to leave open the possibility of both (monks or layman) being commissioned (to preach) by competent authority."[18]

Despite the close connection between preaching and priesthood emphasized by Leo, there were hints of lay preaching possibilities in the centuries following his letter.[19]

The Middle Ages

Historians of preaching are in basic agreement that there were at least two distinct periods and types of preaching in the Middle Ages, (1) the early Carolingian period, characterized by its dependence on the scriptural text and a more informal approach of preaching popularized by Augustine, and (2) the later period beginning with the eleventh century, noted for its enthusiasm for the *vita apostolica* and the beginning of the "schools." This latter period was instrumental in the development of the thematic sermon in the later Middle Ages, which was used for several centuries.

In the Carolingian era religious reform was of great concern to both rulers and clerics, and the clergy sought to reform the populace primarily through sermons, which were preached to the people at Mass after the Gospel reading. These sermons, preached in the vernacular for the most part, were aimed at educating the common people in the beliefs and practices necessary for salvation. Regular preaching was encouraged, and priests were expected to use prepared sermonaries, for example, Gregory the Great's (+604) *Forty Homilies on the Gospels.* Priests who were not well educated in the Scriptures were expected to get assistance from others so that the common people would be able to understand them.[20]

During this earlier period of the Middle Ages there seems to be no evidence that lay preaching had yet reappeared. Preaching was delegated by the bishops to priests, and priests were expected to preach frequently. On occasion deacons were allowed to read a sermon, for example, in the case of a priest's illness.

Brilioth considers the period following the Carolingian reform a creative era in the history of preaching, as contrasted with the Carolingian period, which he describes as more of a reproductive one, drawing its major content from patristic sources. He notes that in this latter period the threefold influence of the Crusades, monasticism, and Scholasticism were interwoven and resulted in a period of preaching that was rich in its enthusiasm and diversity and that gave rise to a highly developed preaching technique, a primary contribution of the late Middle Ages. Interestingly, he does not include the *vita apostolica* among these influences.[21]

13

Lay Preaching Returns

The eleventh to the early thirteenth century was an extraordinarily complex but fruitful time in the history of the Church and quite significant in the history of lay preaching. For lay preaching it was both the best of times and the worst of times. The resurgence of lay preaching was a notable development during the earlier phase, and yet toward the end of this period it was prohibited again.

According to Kenan Osborne, a number of reform movements developed during this period, which although geographically disparate tended to circle around a common theme: the gospel life, or *vita evangelica* (called *vita apostolica* by other authors.) Some of these groups were later considered suspect and declared heretical; others were seen as more acceptable movements and gained a certain status in the perspective of later historians. Characteristic of all of these movements was an energy and enthusiasm for renewal and the fostering of this renewal through preaching and teaching. Laypersons as well as monks and clerics were integral to these reform movements.[22]

The twelfth century is particularly noteworthy in the revival of the lay preaching movement because it was during this period that the preaching bands began to develop all over western Europe. These preachers saw the source of their authority to preach in their faithfulness to living the gospel life. This was a significant change from the criterion used since the fifth century to determine suitability for preaching, that is, ordination or authorization from the appropriate authority. For many twelfth-century preachers the mandate to preach flowed naturally from their commitment to be followers of Christ.[23] These preaching bands included among their numbers laity and monks who were not ordained. Preaching became more detached from a eucharistic setting as the preaching bands moved out of the churches into the public squares of Europe. Although not a new practice, this appears to be a factor that encouraged the resurgence of lay preaching in this period.[24]

Skudlarek describes the lay preaching phenomenon of the twelfth century: "Lay preaching was but one of the more striking manifestations of 'awakening' of the human spirit that affected not only the church, but all of Western civilization during the twelfth century." Laypersons in the Church were becoming more conscious of their dignity and mission as Christian believers. The gulf between clergy and laity had been widening more and more since the Gregorian reform of the eleventh century, although this same reform "was also responsible for awakening in the laity a new sense of their Christian vocation," since monk and layperson alike had been enlisted in the reform of the clergy. Also, during the twelfth century a number of factors, including the Crusades, brought the laity in closer contact with the humanity of Jesus and developed in them a strong desire to live the life that Jesus and his followers, the apostles, lived—the "apostolic life." Gradually, laity became more aware of their call to preach repentance and to proclaim the reign of God. A renewed interest in the gospel with its invitation to come closer to Jesus and to imitate him led some laity to see that the call of preaching the gospel was addressed to them, not only the clergy. Preaching was seen by them to be "more than an office in the church; it was an integral part of the full and complete following of Christ."[25]

Hilkert points out that women were among the laypersons preaching during this period. For example, an abbess of a monastery was permitted to preach, even in a joint monastery of women and men, because she was the superior of the community. Her rank gave her access to the right to preach. The well-known mystic Hildegard of Bingen (+1179), a Benedictine nun of the twelfth century, preached to clergy, laity, monks, nuns, and even ecclesiastical officials.[26]

Before official approval of his order by Pope Innocent III (+1216) in Rome in 1210, Francis, as a layman, along with his band of followers, preached the gospel in the towns throughout the day, returning to his cave at night.[27] Once established as an official order, the Franciscan friars brought back the ideal of the itinerant preachers so characteristic of the preachers in the Gospels and Acts and were later joined by other groups.

The historical data seems to support the view that during this period (eleventh to thirteenth century) the mandate to preach was not tied to ordination alone and that women as well as laymen, in certain circumstances, preached. Authority to preach arose from one's commitment to the gospel and the "charism" to preach, as well as approval from the appropriate ecclesiastical authority.

It is not altogether clear from examining the history of preaching in the Middle Ages whether or not lay women and men who did preach, preached at Eucharist regularly or even at all. It is quite clear that they preached in public places and in gatherings at which they spoke about the teachings of the faith and living a proper moral life; it is not as clear that they preached in the eucharistic assembly. In this era the distinctions between "official" worship and

15

popular devotion were much more blurred than today, and the different types of preaching and teaching were not delineated clearly, either. It is difficult to resolve this question definitively. The significant point is that lay persons were engaged in preaching during this period and did so with enthusiasm and conviction, and in some instances were invited to preach at the request of someone with ecclesiastical authority.

The Fourth Lateran Council

By the time of the Fourth Lateran Council lay preaching was once again prohibited. Preaching was limited to clergy, who were expected to take responsibility for the pastoral care of souls through the exercise of other sacramental offices as well. When the council participants gathered, they were preoccupied with the issue of heresy and sought ways to prevent heretical preaching and teaching. They considered the state of preaching poor, due in part to what they perceived as the unorthodox views put forth by certain lay preachers as well as priests who were not properly prepared. Therefore they decided to put a stop to lay preaching.

> It often happens that bishops by themselves are not sufficient to minister the word of God to the people, especially in large and scattered dioceses. . . . We therefore decree by this general constitution that bishops are to appoint suitable men *(viros)* to carry out with profit this duty of sacred preaching, men who are powerful in word and deed and who will visit with care the peoples entrusted to them in place of the bishops [and] . . . we . . . order that there be appointed in both cathedral and other conventual churches suitable men whom the bishops can have as coadjutors and cooperators not only in the office of preaching but also in hearing confessions and enjoining penances and in other matters which are conducive to the salvation of souls (Can 10).[28]

The council also set up guidelines for the appointment of teachers of grammar and theology at the cathedral and major churches for the proper education of the clergy.

In assessing the position of Innocent III, who presided over the council, regarding lay preaching, Skudlarek uses the phrase "cautious tolerance." Innocent III had no theological objections to lay preaching by an educated lay man but did not view it as a permanent institution that could resolve the problems of poor preaching.

Although ironically he tolerated lay preaching by qualified lay men who were commissioned by the proper authority, Innocent III understood the nature of preaching primarily as a teaching office in the Church and closely related to the ministry of the sacraments. He was also keenly aware of the problems in the past quarter century with heretical groups of lay preachers, even though he was instrumental in reconciling some of them to the Church and allowed them to continue preaching (e.g., converted Waldenses and Humiliati).[29]

The Council of Trent

The Council of Trent solidified the distinction between the clergy and laity with regard to ministry, especially in the administration of the sacraments. It called for the establishment of seminaries for the education of clergy and clearly spelled out the rights and responsibilities of clergy regarding the sacraments, including a new emphasis on the proper use of the Bible in preaching. A major emphasis of the council was a discussion of the seven sacraments and the role of holy orders as the appropriate access to the right to administer the sacraments. By this time there was no hint of participation by laity in preaching. Lay preaching was forbidden. Preaching was identified exclusively with clergy.

Norris points out that "from the Council of Trent to the promulgation of the 1917 Code . . . preaching required ordination, but more importantly, canonical mission, either by means of office or special faculty."[30]

The Twentieth Century

The 1917 Code of Canon Law states emphatically that lay preaching is prohibited. Canon 1342 §1 states that the "faculty to preach should be given only to priests or deacons, and not to other clerics unless for a reasonable cause, according to the judgment of the Ordinary, and in individual cases." Canon 1342 §2 speaks of the role of laity explicitly: ". . . and all laymen, religious as well, are forbidden to preach in church."[31]

Between that time and the promulgation of the 1983 revised code, two well-known exceptions to the 1917 directives against lay preaching had been made. The first was in response to the request of the German bishops in the 1970s, who asked permission for qualified lay persons to preach in the churches in Germany due to the shortage of priests. In 1973 permission was granted on an experimental basis from the Apostolic See via a letter signed by John Cardinal Wright. Summarizing its content, James Provost writes:

> Laypersons could be authorized to give a homily at Sunday celebrations without a priest, with no mention given of the homily being pre-selected by the bishop or pastor. Laypersons could also be authorized to preach even during Mass when the celebrant was "physically or morally prevented from fulfilling this function." . . . In addition to such necessity, the same faculty could be given on particular occasions when it would be useful for the layperson to preach during Mass.[32]

Provost comments that, in regard to the last sentence above, similar permissions were granted the Swiss, Austrian, and East German bishops.

The second major exception permitting lay preaching during a eucharistic liturgy is *The Directory for Masses with Children* (1973), which states: "With the consent of the pastor or rector of the church, one of the adults may speak to the children after the gospel, especially if the priest finds it difficult to adapt himself to the mentality of the children" (n. 24).[33]

The 1983 revised Code of Canon Law, which states explicitly that laypersons may preach in a church or oratory, will be discussed in full in chapter three of this essay.

Lessons from History

The late medieval historian Walter Principe, well known by colleagues for his scholarship and commitment to the study of history, frequently spoke about how the study of history can free us from the tyranny of the present.[34] Despite the long-term presence of many practices that we experience in the present, chances are that when we take a close look at history we will learn that it was not always done *that* way.

Reflection on the history of lay preaching leads us to the following conclusions: (1) Lay preaching has been a practice in several different periods in the history of the Church. There is evidence that some of this preaching was liturgical preaching. (2) Lay preaching has been done by both women and men. However, women were excluded from lay preaching at times when lay men were still permitted to preach. (3) Authorization for lay preaching has been approached differently in each era. (4) The reasons for the prohibition of lay preaching at various times are complex and included political, social, cultural, and ecclesiastical as well as theological influences. (5) At present, lay preaching is permitted under certain circumstances by Church law. (6) Lay preaching is growing as an accepted practice in some segments of the contemporary Roman Catholic Church.

The complexity of this history alone calls us to humility and requires that we stay open. No strong statement against lay preaching will hold up by itself against the overwhelming evidence of lay preaching in the history of the Church. Lay preachers are as diverse as ordained preachers and cannot be stereotyped. Some have been influential in their communities and proclaimed a gospel that invited people to a deeper following of Jesus; others have had their own agenda and preached in ways that caused division and disharmony.

Having painted a picture of the historical movement of lay preaching in the Church from its inception, we will now examine the major theological and liturgical considerations that have had a significant impact on the growing interest in and practice of lay preaching in the contemporary Roman Catholic Church.

2 Mapping the Theological Terrain

Considering the issue of lay preaching, particularly liturgical preaching, requires not only a sense of its historical movement from the New Testament period to the present but an understanding of the contemporary theological and liturgical environment, which has created new questions and concerns for the Church in our time. In this chapter we will examine some of the questions and concerns most pertinent to the topic of lay preaching.

As Sandra Schneiders points out, considering the historical data alone is insufficient for the study of lay preaching. In terms of examining the New Testament data, she says, "The real question is not *whether* such or such a thing was done or not done by Jesus or the early Church but *why*." She then speaks of the limited but real value of the historical data: "First . . . the facts we uncover orient us correctly to the significant questions that relate to our present concerns. . . . Secondly, the historical facts can help to relativize convictions that have been erroneously absolutized in the course of our long history as an institution."[35]

For Schneiders the real value of historical data is not the gathering of the facts but "the task of theological interpretation in which a genuine fusion of horizons, that is, of our contemporary horizon with the horizon of the earliest Christian experience, takes place. Within this newly established horizon we must raise our own questions and find our own answers."[36]

The Laity's Mandate

In raising "our own questions" and finding "our own answers," a number of contemporary theologians have not only sifted through the historical data about preaching but have begun also to explore the *whys* of lay preaching for our time, offering us the fruits of their theological reflection. A majority of these theologians agree that the statements of Vatican II, acknowledging the inclusion of the laity in the mission of the Church and asserting that this call comes through the initiative and action of God in baptism, represent a qualitatively different ecclesiology from at least the four hundred years previous to the council. This change in the way of envisioning the Church has far-reaching effects on the issue of lay preaching.

Although there is a lack of consistency in the council documents about the relationship of clergy and laity, the importance given to the laity's mandate and inclusion in the preaching of the gospel is highlighted throughout and represents a significant change from previous approaches. A few statements from the documents of Vatican II illustrate this new emphasis:

The Decree on the Apostolate of Lay People *(Apostolicam actuositatem)* states that by virtue of their initiation into the Christian community, laypeople are called to be apostles; their mandate comes directly from God in Christ: "From the fact of their union with Christ the head flows the laymen's right and duty to be apostles. Inserted as they are in the Mystical Body of Christ by baptism and strengthened by the power of the Holy Spirit in confirmation, it is by the Lord himself that they are assigned to the apostolate."[37]

According to the Dogmatic Constitution on Divine Revelation *(Dei verbum)*, the word of God is given to the whole Church. "Sacred Tradition and sacred Scripture make up a single sacred deposit of the Word of God, which is entrusted to the Church."[38]

In the Decree on the Church's Missionary Activity *(Ad gentes divinitus)*, we are told that evangelization is the work of all God's people: "Since the whole Church is missionary . . . the work of evangelization [is] the fundamental task of the people of God."[39]

The Mission of the Church

With some convergence of the biblical, liturgical, and catechetical movements in the first half of the twentieth century, the description of the Church's mission was increasingly articulated in terms of kerygma (the proclamation of God's saving work in Christ) through such terms as proclamation or preaching for describing the mandate to all who had been initiated. The call of all the baptized was that of proclaiming the wonderful works of God through all the means at their disposal, that is, the witness of their lives, works of charity and justice, catechetical instruction, and so on.

By the time of Vatican II (1962–65), influenced by the writings of theologians such as Yves Congar (+1995) and Karl Rahner (+1984), the Church's mission of announcing the saving work of God in Christ was considered first and foremost a ministry of the word. Laity as well as clergy were called to participate in this mission of proclamation, both in word and deed. Understanding the Christ-event as *the* word, which has been uttered, Rahner viewed the Church as the community called to proclaim this one word to all: "The Church is the abiding presence of that primal sacramental word of definitive grace, which Christ is in the world, effecting what is uttered by uttering it in sign."[40]

> As the community of those who hear this word and believe, the Church becomes the sign of the fact that God has irrevocably com- municated with humankind in the salvific action of Christ and con- tinues to offer the message of salvation to all. This continuous rhythm of the speaking of God in history and the hearing of this word by the community of believers who respond in a life expressing this belief, is what makes the church a living, dynamic reality. . . . The task of the Church, the community of those who have heard and believed, is to continue to utter that word in all that it is and does in time, in his- tory.[41]

While acknowledging that Vatican II did not completely over- come its ambiguity in the way it distinguished between clergy and laity, David Power illustrates the impact of the council's recognition of the laity's inclusion in the Church's mission:

> The truly singular thing about the teaching of the Second Vatican Council is the self-image of the church adopted by the *Constitution on the Church*. The image of the People of God which prevails today has far-reaching effects on the way in which the respective missions of clerics and laity are conceived and lived. . . . [I]t is the church as God's People which receives and bears Christ's mission and is his sacrament in the world. The primary mission is not that given to the hierarchy. . . . Christ's mission and Spirit are given to the body of the church so that laity and clergy share in their respective ways in the one mission of God's People and in the triple office of Jesus Christ as Priest, Prophet and King.[42]

This new emphasis on the laity's mandate to participate in the mission of the Church and in the threefold office of Jesus the Christ has significant implications for lay involvement in the ministry of the word, specifically preaching, which is so central in the overall mission of the Church. By highlighting the significance of the laity in proclaiming the gospel through their lives, words, and works, Vatican II is considered a real turning point in paving the way for discussion, once again, about the practice of lay preaching in the Church.

Suitability for Preaching

One implication of this new ecclesiology of Vatican II, which assumes that laity are integrally involved in the mission of the Church, is the need to envision new ways for determining suitability for the preaching ministry. This preoccupation with suitability seems to be one of the main roadblocks to lay preaching today. Who is a suitable candidate or who is fit to preach, and how is that determined?

The question of suitability is a major theme running through the historical controversies surrounding lay preaching, especially liturgical preaching. In judging suitability or fitness, the emphasis at times has been on charism or competency, such as in the New Testament period and the early Church; at other times it seemed to be more centered on rank and/or gender, such as in the third and fourth centuries; in the early Middle Ages the question of suitability for preaching was focused on office, on persons who held superior rank or were part of the clerical order; still at other times, especially during the period of the *vita apostolica,* discussed above, what was considered most important was that a person live a life committed to the gospel. In the later Middle Ages orders and a canonical mission or a special faculty to preach were the necessary prerequisites. Often in the periods mentioned above the criteria for suitability included several of the different emphases in combination.

Since the time of the Council of Trent to the present the strong accent in determining suitability for the preaching ministry has been on ordination. Only the ordained are deemed suitable for preaching, especially liturgical preaching. Laity who do preach at eucharistic liturgy and in other liturgical contexts still do so by way of exception. Other forms of lay preaching require specific authorization as well.[43]

Many believe that this criterion of ordination is no longer satisfactory or even acceptable in the present context, in which many laypersons are theologically adept as well as actively involved in ministries that lend themselves to preaching regularly. Those who question the requirement of ordination as the sole criterion for determining who may preach, especially at eucharistic liturgy, contend that not only does it not fit the changed ecclesiology expressed and lived out in the Church since Vatican II, but it fails to take into account the present needs of God's people for hearing the word preached. They regret, too, that the rich and diverse gifts of laywomen and laymen committed to proclaiming God's word will be lost if this limitation persists. Given the above considerations, it seems that the whole issue of suitability needs to be reframed in light of present reality.

Baptism as the Basis for the Mandate to Preach

Baptism as the first of the sacraments of initiation into the Christian community is recognized by bishops and theologians alike as the basis for participation in the Church's mission of proclamation of the gospel to all. Vatican II as well as postconciliar statements are replete with this notion. For example, the 1976 statement "The Role of Women in Evangelization" states: "Every Christian, of whatever sex, age or situation, is called to be an apostle. In virture of their baptism, all Christians are not merely called and made capable of belief, they are also called to radiate and transmit it."[44]

It is baptism that bring us into communion with the whole Christ. It is baptism that gives us a mandate, reminiscent of that of the woman at the well (John 4), to recognize, believe, and rejoice in the marvelous works of God in our midst and then to invite others to experience the unconditional love of God in Christ for themselves.

Mary Collins suggests that by examining the theological language and ritual of the baptismal liturgy throughout our history as a Christian community we can understand more profoundly its real significance. Her analysis gives us a new way to look at the question of suitability or fitness for preaching the word of God.

According to Collins, the Church's sacramental praxis, as *theologia prima*, should provide the data for systematic theology, or *theologia secunda*. She bemoans the fact that much of the work of systematic theology fails to take seriously the practice of liturgy as a source for its theologizing. Collins contends that because at times aspects of this liturgical tradition do not fit into the conceptual framework of systematics it is therefore dismissed. In looking at the issue at hand —that of determining the foundation for the mandate to preach— she states:

> Such selectivity in dealing with the data of the tradition of public prayer has contributed to the present theological impasse in the matter of whether the authentic sacramental foundation for the ministry of preaching is ordination. The Church's faith is fuller and deeper than what has been given systematic form since the twelfth century.[45]

Collins points out that the baptismal liturgy itself has remained quite consistent throughout our history despite the major changes in the social, political, and ecclesiastical worlds surrounding its celebration. For that reason it remains a constant witness to the meaning and implications of initiation into the Christian community.

In her study Collins analyzes two liturgical moments of the celebration of baptism, St. Cyril's (+386/387) reflection on the baptismal praxis of fourth-century Jerusalem and the baptismal liturgy of the Frankish realm in the eighth century during the reign of Charlemagne. After examining these two ritual moments and the way the theological language in these liturgies expresses the theology of the sacrament of baptism, she concludes: "The Church's liturgical tradition shows that the original insight into notions of sacred fitness, empowerment by the Holy Spirit and transformation into the living image of the Savior arose in the context of celebrations of Christian baptism."[46]

Collins notes that this language was later applied primarily to the recipients of holy orders and was used to assert the long-held bond between orders and preaching, which is still operative today. But for Collins this reference to the ordained is secondary and derivative in the prayer life of the Church and may be more of an ideological statement that gives little credence to the nature of liturgy as the primary source for systematic theology.[47]

Collins' study leads her to the conclusion that

> we can and must question the assertion that the sacrament of holy orders is the adequate foundation for the ministry of the Word, and acknowledge, rather, that it *is in holy baptism that the Church can recognize the radical capacity and the fundamental imperative for the preaching ministry.*[48]

On the basis of this analysis it is baptism, then, that makes one *suitable* for the ministry of preaching.

Preaching at Eucharist

Without a doubt the most problematic area in the discussion of lay preaching today is that of the suitability or fitness of laypersons to preach at the Eucharist. At the present time the preaching of the homily at Eucharist is limited to the ordained.[49] This issue has a long history. Although the association of preaching at Eucharist with orders was clearly affirmed at the Fourth Lateran Council, it was not until Trent that this bond was solidified. From that period to and including the present there has been little change, despite the new openness of the 1983 revised Code of Canon Law toward lay preaching in general.

Two major theological concerns are at the center of this discussion: (1) the relationship of orders and Eucharist and (2) the nature of the homily.

The first issue concerns the Church's long-standing tradition between orders and preaching at Eucharist. The key question in this concern is one regarding the integrity of Eucharist, that is, does the presider need to be the one to preach the homily given the intimate connection between word and sacrament in the celebration of the Eucharist?

The council documents as well as postconciliar statements have made it clear that the preaching of the liturgical homily at Eucharist is a high priority in the ministry of the ordained. Describing the priesthood as essentially a ministry of the word with liturgical preaching of the homily as its high point, the document on the ministry of priests considers this ministry of the word, especially the homily at Eucharist, as the "first task" of priests as co-workers with the bishops.[50]

In addressing this relationship, most liturgical theologians see this close bond flowing from the nature of ordination itself. For example, William Skudlarek states that

> priests are ordained precisely to the ministry of word and sacrament. The Christian community, acting through the bishop, calls them to this ministry because it recognizes in them an ability to communicate the word of God to the people of God and to lead that community in prayer. If a priest were regularly, or frequently, to hand this ministry over to others, one could legitimately ask if he should continue to serve the church in the ministry of the ordained priesthood.[51]

Skudlarek upholds two values in creative tension in his discussion of this issue. Given the nature of this close relationship between ordination and preaching, he suggests that the ordinary preacher at the Eucharist is the presider or another ordained person who is con-celebrating. At the same time he supports the right and need of laypersons to preach occasionally at the Eucharist. Skudlarek urges that rather than substitute lay preachers at Eucharist on a regular basis the Church needs to address the real issue, "which is not whether or not lay people should be able to preach in the liturgical assembly, but whether or not the church will maintain its policy of ordaining only unmarried men to the ministry of word and sacra-ment."[52]

For Skudlarek, the significant contribution of lay preaching is that fresh voices will be heard; the assembly will benefit from expe-riencing the word of God proclaimed in a new way. "Lay preachers speaking out of their experience, can show how the word intersects with and interprets those human realities which priests, by their training and life-style, simply cannot or, for the most part, do not know of at first hand."[53]

Some others who admit the value of and need for lay preaching, even at Eucharist, also would not support the practice of lay preach-ing at Eucharist as an ordinary practice. For example, J. Frank Henderson proposes the use of laypeople as extraordinary minis-ters of preaching at the Eucharist since there is precedent for this in past practice as well as in the present practice and law of the Church, for example, in Masses celebrated with children and the experiment allowed the West German bishops in the early 1970s. He points out that whenever a deacon or a priest who is not the presider of the liturgy preaches, he, too, is considered an extraordi-nary minister of preaching.

According to Henderson, the lay extraordinary ministers would have to meet certain requirements, which would include their in-volvement with their congregation as an active member, in addition to the various competencies needed to preach well. They would preach in two types of situations: "a) when the ordinary presbyter minister is physically absent; and b) when he is morally absent." They would exercise their preaching in the name of the Church and would be officially delegated in some way. In offering suggestions for allowing a variety of preachers Henderson's purpose is to serve the gathered assembly well: "The good of the liturgical assembly should always be the goal, and it is to be hoped that this matter would not bog down in legalism, distrust, authoritarianism or anti-clericalism."[54]

David Power approaches the issue from a somewhat different vantage point. While he recognizes the close relationship between the liturgical presider and the entire eucharistic movement from word through sacrament, he sees no inherent conflict between this relationship and the call of the laity to exercise their gifts in the assembly. Power believes that "[t]he one who proclaims the eucharistic prayer . . . must be able to proclaim and interpret the scripture for the community" but recognizes that the precise way that this preaching takes shape in relationship to the other participating members of the worshiping community is open to exploration and new discovery.

> There is no necessary conflict between the ordained minister's presidency of the liturgy . . . and the participation of the laity in sacramental and word ministries. The call of the laity to minister, as it is taking shape within our time, needs to be properly integrated into a liturgy in which the presider's role is also taking on a new shape. . . . A firm presidency . . . through which the interpretation of the word carries over into the proclamation of the blessing and the offer of the sacrament to the community is quite compatible with a multiple exercise of charisms of proclamation and interpretation by other members of the community.[55]

Power highlights what he calls "the real issue" about liturgical preaching by laypersons. For him it is

> the demand put upon the church to allow the gifts of the Spirit given to the baptized to be exercised properly. The ordering of the assembly cannot be determined by the principles of law alone. The discernment and exercise of spiritual gifts have their part to play as well. Today, it is evident that many of the baptized are gifted and called to present and interpret the meaning of God's word, as proclaimed in the scriptures and active in the lives of the faithful. *Room must be made, therefore, to allow lay persons to give the homily at the eucharist and other liturgical services.*[56]

Mary Collins' study of baptism leads her to similar conclusions about sacramentality and Eucharist. For her the baptismal liturgy suggests that "sacramentality is a quality of the whole *ecclesia*, the community of those who are being transformed slowly, by God's power, into living images of the saving Christ. It is the whole Church together that makes the Eucharist."[57]

Drawing from this understanding, Collins raises an important point with serious ramifications for this first theological concern.

Since Eucharist is an act of the whole Church, the presider is acting as someone *within* rather than *over* the community of believers. She holds that it is therefore possible to envision and create new models for understanding the relationship of liturgical presidency and sacramentality. In fact, she says,

> Ecclesial experience confirms that it is possible for the one who presides within the liturgical assembly by office to engage another believer to lead them all together into deeper communion with the mystery of Christ by the power of the Word, and that this collaborative ordering does not fracture the sacrament of unity. Perhaps the question is whether the presidency of the ordained minister in the liturgical assembly inevitably involves prelacy or may just as authentically manifest collaboration within the one Body.[58]

Collins believes that resolution of this concern will not come until the theology of baptism and that of ordination are examined together within the theological community. Until that time, she believes, those who want to find firm ground for collaboration with laypersons in the full preaching ministry will be kept in a defensive position. She is convinced that "the witness of the baptismal liturgy shows convincingly that the burden of proof should rest rather with those who want to disqualify the laity as a class from preaching in any or all of its forms."[59]

John Baldovin would support Collins in her view of the presider as acting within rather than over the community. In an address to the Catholic Theological Society of America Baldovin discussed the question of ministerial leadership of the Eucharist. He believes that among other characteristics needed for effective ministerial leadership is that of shared leadership:

> It is clear in the documents of the reform that ministerial leadership of the eucharist (and other liturgical acts) is not considered a solo activity. The model . . . proposed by the *General Instruction of the Roman Missal,* not to mention the text of the liturgy itself, presupposed a co-ordinated ministerial leadership. . . . [L]eadership is a shared activity in the Roman Rite and the perceived dominance of the ordained presider is an anomaly that needs to be rectified—more in practice than in theory. . . . [A] desirable charism in the ordained leader of the community is the ability to share leadership.[60]

The second major theological concern that affects the choice of who may preach at the Eucharist is the nature of the homily. From a theological-liturgical perspective, what is a homily and what is its purpose?

The Constitution on the Sacred Liturgy gives the basic description of a homily, and several postconciliar documents expand that description. The revised General Introduction to the Lectionary for Mass integrates these previous descriptions and provides the basis for the definition in the 1983 revised Code of Canon Law. The introduction describes the homily as follows:

> In the homily, the mysteries of faith and the guiding principles of the Christian life are expounded from the sacred text in the course of the liturgical year. As part of the liturgy of the word it has been frequently and, since the promulgation of the Liturgy Constitution of Vatican II, most strongly, recommended; in some instances it is obligatory. Normally it should be delivered by the person presiding. What the homily sets out to achieve is to make of the word of God proclaimed, together with the eucharistic liturgy, "as it were the proclamation of God's wonderful works in the history of salvation, which is the mystery of Christ." For the paschal mystery of Christ, which is proclaimed in the readings and in the homily, is accomplished by the sacrifice of the Mass. Christ is always present and active in the preaching of his Church.
>
> The homily, therefore, whether it be an exposition of the word of Scripture which has been read, or of another liturgical text, should lead the community of believers to active celebration of the eucharist, so that "they should hold fast in their lives to what they have grasped in faith." The word of God which is read and the Church's celebration will draw greater effectiveness from this living exposition if the homily be truly the fruit of reflection, if it be properly prepared, not too long, nor too short, and if it take everyone present into account, even children and the uneducated.
>
> At a concelebrated Mass, the homily is usually given by the chief celebrant or by one of the concelebrants.[61]

A number of theological-liturgical assumptions are present in this statement: (1) attention to the liturgical year is important; (2) a homily should expound the mysteries of faith and give guidance for living the Christian life; (3) the sacred texts used in the liturgy are to form the basis of the homily; (4) a homily is an important part of the eucharistic liturgy; (5) the homily is normally delivered by the one presiding; (6) the homily and the eucharistic action are part of one movement in proclaiming God's wonderful works; (7) the paschal mystery is to be proclaimed in the homily; (8) Christ is present in the preaching of the homily; (9) the homily should help the worshiping assembly to enter into the eucharistic action so that their lives are formed by what they heard at Eucharist; (10) the preacher's preparation includes time for reflection if the homily is to be fruitful; (11) the needs of the congregation are important, and the preacher needs to be aware of those needs in preparing the homily.

A close analysis of this description of a homily discloses some ambiguity. For example, is the homily primarily a time for "expounding" the mysteries of the faith or rather a time to form the assembly by the word so they can better enter into the eucharistic action? How are the needs of the faithful discerned and by whom? What constitutes proper preparation of the homily?

In relation to the first question, this description of the homily takes a middle road between the two perspectives. On the one hand it speaks of the homily as a proclamatory moment that serves to evoke a response in faith; on the other hand it speaks of the homily as a time to expound the principles for living a good moral life. In a sense, this description is a compromise that tries to capture the best of both perspectives. However, by lacking real clarity about the main purpose of a homily, this description serves to cloud the issue and brings little resolution to both the nature of the homily and what it is trying to effect in the assembly.

Regarding the second example of ambiguity in this description about who discerns the needs of the community and how, it would be a helpful exercise to query preachers about how many of them include members of their congregation in a discussion of what they need and want from the preaching of a homily. If the preacher alone tries to discern the needs of the faithful, chances are that many of those needs perceived to be important to the members of the congregation could be missed. This implies, too, that preaching is an act of the preacher alone rather a dialogic event that requires the participation of the congregation.

In trying to determine what constitutes proper homily preparation, it is difficult for the preacher to answer that question alone. Only in dialogue with the listeners in the congregation over an extended period of time will a preacher be able to determine what is needed for effective preaching, and, hence, good preparation in the concrete situation.

To further our analysis of the nature of the homily, it might be helpful to center our discussion on a major area of concern that underlies some of the ambiguity in the above description, that is, whether a homily is more properly associated with the genre of interpretation or exposition. Is the homily more appropriately a word that interprets the sacred texts (scriptural and liturgical) and the experience of the congregation in that light, or is the homily a word of instruction about or exposition of the teachings of the faith?

Throughout the history of preaching, this question has been discussed and debated endlessly. It is not surprising that it continues to receive much attention, since decisions about who may preach often have been made in light of the answer to this question. At those times when preaching was viewed as primarily a way of evoking the faith of those present, when preaching interpreted the meaning of the life of the community in light of the word proclaimed through the entire eucharistic action, it seems that preachers were called forth on the basis of their charism to announce the good news faithfully and enthusiastically with conviction. At other times, when preaching was seen as primarily a way of teaching or instructing the faithful, the authority to preach was limited to bishop and clergy, who were seen as the true teachers of the faith. It was understood that those who taught in the name of the Church were those who had that authority by right of their office.

In an article about preaching by laity, James Wallace makes a strong plea for bringing into greater prominence the approach to the homily as described in the United States bishops' document *Fulfilled in Your Hearing*. The basic understanding of the homily central to this document is "a scriptural interpretation of human existence which enables a community to recognize God's active presence, to respond to that presence in faith through liturgical word and gesture, and beyond the liturgical assembly, through a life lived in conformity with the Gospel."[62] Wallace expresses both disappointment and surprise that the 1988 proposed guidelines for lay preaching prepared by the United States bishops did not draw more from that document's approach to the homily.[63]

The description of the homily found in *Fulfilled in Your Hearing* takes seriously the experience of the gathered assembly as that experience is touched and interpreted by the Scriptures and other liturgical texts of the day. It takes seriously, too, the active presence of God in the whole liturgical action and moves the believing community to living lives committed to the gospel outside of that celebration.

Wallace contends that "this document offers not only a new paradigm for the homily but also the basis for a more inclusive group of preachers."[64] Here the preacher "is not first and foremost a teacher. Rather, the preacher is one who is an interpreter, a mediator of meaning, a listener; one who in the act of speaking represents both the assembly in its daily existence and the God revealed by Jesus Christ in the power of the Spirit who is active and present now."[65]

The difference between viewing the homily primarily as an instructive act or as an interpretive one appears to flow from contrasting views of revelation. The former approach puts more emphasis on what is given in the Scriptures, in tradition, in Church teaching; the latter approach gives more weight to the here-and-now experience of the gathered assembly and how the Scriptures, liturgy, tradition, and Church teachings have something to say to their lives now. Wallace develops this idea further and concludes that approaching the homily primarily as an interpretive act leaves more room for inviting and including a greater variety of preachers, which would enrich the Church and nourish God's people.[66]

Clearly, *Fulfilled in Your Hearing* does much to further our understanding of the homily. It also provides insight into the integral role of the assembly in the whole act of worship. Its theological presumptions go to the heart of the changed ecclesiology described above and give added credibility to the need for recognizing the mandate of all the baptized to participate fully in the ministry of the word.

In this chapter we have tried to explore some of the more significant concerns raised by the contemporary theological and liturgical environment, that is, the laity's mandate to participate in the mission of the Church: the proclamation of the gospel; the issue of suitability for preaching; baptism as the basis for the mandate to preach; and preaching at Eucharist, including an examination of the relationship of orders and preaching and the nature of the homily. Many of these issues have been addressed in major theological and liturgical journals, expanding and deepening the questions merely touched upon here. This discussion—related directly to the issue of lay preaching—is a small beginning and needs to continue if there is to be any resolution of the serious conflicts that keep us from recognizing the place that lay preaching has, once again, in the contemporary Roman Catholic community of faith. To move these questions to a more practical level of decision making, the Christian community needs to reflect on them together in a spirit of discernment and inquiry, bringing to the forefront the actual lived experience of preaching in the gathered community of faith and always keeping in mind the priority of the community's need for good and effective preaching.

In chapter 3 we will examine the 1983 revised Code of Canon Law to gain an understanding of its perspective on the question of lay preaching. Since recent documents and directives from Rome have given Church law an increasingly important role in determining who may preach in liturgical settings and under what circumstances, it is important that we look closely at canon law in context to understand its intent and to capture the spirit of its directives.[67]

3 Perspective of the 1983 Code of Canon Law

Writing shortly before the implementation of the 1983 revised Code of Canon Law, James Provost notes that with a renewed view of the Church following Vatican II we can benefit from new insights into the way law works in our Church. Recognizing the appropriate limits of law and at the same time the active role of the Spirit working within the whole body of Christ, he urges us to keep in mind that the sources of Church law are broader than the Code of Canon Law alone:

> The sources of Church law today include the 1917 Code, the documents of the Second Vatican Council, postconciliar decrees that look to implementing the Council and the renewal that carries its name. Church law is also found in liturgical law, chiefly the norms at the beginning of the various rituals; it exists in particular law, in special indults or permissions given to various parts of the Church, and in the customs of Church people.[68]

In the previous chapter we examined some of the more significant theological and liturgical issues that pertain to the question of lay preaching. Included in that study was a look at some of the sources of Church law noted by Provost: Vatican II documents inviting us to a renewed understanding of the laity's participation in the ministry of the word; postconciliar decrees and practices allowing for the possibility of lay preaching; a consideration of the needs of the People of God for good and effective preaching, which is the primary concern of those responsible for the ministry of the word. In the present chapter we will concentrate on another source of Church law, the 1983 revised Code of Canon Law, to see what light it sheds on the topic of lay preaching, especially preaching in church and liturgical preaching. Where it is appropriate we will compare and contrast the revised code with the code of 1917. We will begin by citing the pertinent canons and describing their contents; then we will look at various interpretations of certain canons that could lead the discussion in different directions; finally, we will draw some conclusions based on the data outlined above.

The Ministry of the Divine Word

The canons that are at the center of our discussion can be found in Book III of the code, "The Teaching Office of the Church, Title I, The Ministry of the Divine Word." Particular attention will be given to those canons in chapter 1, "Preaching the Word of God," that have direct implications for the issue of lay preaching: Canons 766 and 767.

Canons 756–61 describe in some detail those who have the responsibility for the ministry of the word in the Church. After speaking about the responsibility of the pope and the college of bishops for preaching the gospel to the whole Church, these canons proceed to discuss others who share in that responsibility. Beginning with the traditional presupposition that individual bishops are the moderators of the entire ministry of the word in their churches, the code continues by stating that priests are cooperators with the bishops in proclaiming the gospel; deacons are to serve God's people in this ministry of the word in union with the bishop and the *presbyterium*. Members of religious institutes and laypersons, too, are called upon to share in the proclamation of the gospel. Finally, Canon 761 highlights preaching and catechetical instruction as two primary ways of exercising the ministry of the word and, in addition, stresses the importance of using a variety of appropriate means of proclaiming the gospel in different milieus.

It is Canon 759 that provides the context for our discussion of lay preaching. A new canon that had no parallel in the 1917 code, this canon states explicitly what Vatican II highlighted in a number of documents:

> In virtue of their baptism and confirmation lay members of the Christian faithful are witnesses to the gospel message by word and by example of a Christian life; they can also be called upon to cooperate with the bishop and presbyters in the exercise of the ministry of the word (Can. 759).[69]

James Coriden points out that this canon makes a distinction between the "obligation and privilege of witnessing to the gospel, incumbent on every baptized Christian and the more public and official 'ministry of the word.'" He comments that "it is most appropriate that they *(laity)* be called upon to share in the ministry of the word along with the bishop and presbyters."[70]

Preaching the Word of God

After this general discussion of those who have responsibility for the ministry of the word, Canons 762–72 focus on the topic of preaching, the first of the two primary ways of exercising the ministry of the word. "Preaching" in these canons can be understood as the different forms of proclamation of the word in church or in a similar setting, such as a retreat or a mission. In the present code preaching is distinguished from catechetical formation, which is treated in chapter 2. The importance of preaching and its treatment in this code of 1983 is in marked contrast to the 1917 code. According to Provost, in the previous code

> [s]pecific norms on preaching were . . . sandwiched between norms on divine worship and benefices [and] appeared . . . after the lengthy treatment of sacraments and sacred times and places, as part of the norms on the ecclesiastical magisterium. Preaching the divine Word covered three chapters: catechetical instruction, sacred conferences ("preaching" in our sense), and sacred missions.
>
> The canons on preaching did not stand out as setting a major tone for the Church's law or pastoral practice, nor did they look to liturgical preaching in any major way. Their major focus was on testing the competence, orthodoxy and morals of the preacher, and in controlling who could preach and where they could do this.[71]

This new importance of preaching in the present code is highlighted in Canon 762.

> Since the people of God are first brought together by the word of the living God, which it is altogether proper to require from the mouth of priests, sacred ministers are to value greatly the task of preaching since among their principal duties is the proclaiming of the gospel of God to all (Can. 762).

For Provost, this canon contains two basic affirmations: (1) "Preaching is central to the reality of the Church itself, . . . is at the very core of Church life"; (2) "preaching is a primary duty of sacred ministers."[72]

Several other canons speak about the ministers of preaching, describing who has an obligation to preach and who is permitted to preach.

Lay Preaching

Canon 766 is most significant to any discussion of lay preaching, since it reopens doors for lay preaching that have been closed formally since the thirteenth century by the directives of the Fourth Lateran Council.

> Laypersons can be admitted to preach in a church or oratory if it is necessary in certain circumstances or if it is useful in particular cases according to the prescriptions of the conference of bishops and with due regard for can. 767 §1 (Can. 766).

Coriden notes that in providing "a broad warrant for lay preaching," this canon "is a complete about-face from the stern prohibition of Canon 1342, §2 of the 1917 code,"[73] which forbade any layperson to preach in church.

In describing the laity to whom this canon refers, Provost points out that in this particular canon "laypersons" includes all who are not ordained, thus "religious," who are not deacons or presbyters, are bound by the same directives as all other laity regarding preaching, as are seminarians, who are not yet ordained.[74] Canonists generally agree that the basis of this right of laypersons to preach in church is their initiation into the Christian community through baptism and confirmation and that the authorization required to preach, "according to the provisions of the Episcopal Conference," is for good order to insure the integrity of the preaching ministry.

In addressing the type of authorization necessary for lay preaching, Provost concludes that it is not a specific *faculty* (such as ordained receive through ordination) that is required for laypersons to preach in church but rather *permission* from the appropriate authority. Although not explicitly stated in this canon, the presumption is that the permission would come from the pastor or church rector, as Canon 767 §4 indicates.[75]

Presently in the United States the issue of authorization for lay preaching is problematic, since there are no approved national guidelines and thus no uniform national policy. In the 1988 proposed guidelines for lay preaching drafted by the National Conference of Catholic Bishops, authorization from the diocesan bishop was deemed necessary for a layperson to preach. However, in the absence of approval by Rome the question of authorization is unclear.

Provost describes the acceptable procedure to follow in the absence of episcopal norms regarding lay preaching in church: "If there are no episcopal conference norms in this regard, the diocesan bishop can establish rules concerning preaching (Canon 772, §1). If he has done so, they must be followed. If he has not done so, then a determination must be made by the rector of the church."[76] This topic will be pursued in more depth in the next chapter.

Considering under what conditions lay preaching can be permitted according to Canon 766, Provost notes that the provisions of necessity and usefulness are not really anything extraordinary. "For example, the combination of these two factors is found elsewhere in the Code as conditioning the incardination of clerics (Canon 269, §1), the policies of associations of the faithful (Canon 304, §1), etc. In other words, they are not exceptional, but rather express the need to be attentive to practical considerations in deciding to permit laypersons to preach in church."[77] He develops this point further by referring to moments in the recent past in which these conditions have prevailed and called for the implementation of lay preaching, for example, a joint synod of German dioceses in the early 1970s addressing the problem of shortage of priests.

John Huels cites the policy of the Canadian bishops as a good example of what is meant by situations of necessity and usefulness. According to the Canadian bishops, lay preaching is authorized as follows: "1) When there is no priest or deacon who can converse in the language of the people; 2) When the liturgy of the word is celebrated without a priest or deacon; 3) When seminarians who have begun their studies in theology are sent to parishes as part of their pastoral formation; 4) When certain circumstances require the participation of lay persons (financial questions, special appeals, special circumstances); 5) When the diocesan bishop judges it opportune."[78]

Liturgical Preaching: The Homily

Most of the present discussion about lay preaching is related to Canon 767. This new canon is directly influenced by several Vatican II documents; for example, *Sacrosanctum concilium* considers the homily "preeminent" (no. 52), *Dei verbum* notes that it is "reserved to a priest or deacon" (no. 24); and *Inter oecumenici* acknowledges that it is "part of the liturgy itself" (nos. 53–55). Canon 767 is the most problematic canon in terms of lay preaching because it sets a limitation that seems to contradict the new openness of Canon 766. In addition, Canon 767 lacks clarity about the meaning of the terms "homily" and "liturgy." Thus it is a subject of confusion and disagreement among many. The entire canon reads as follows:

> §1 Among the forms of preaching the homily is preeminent; it is a part of the liturgy itself and is reserved to a priest or to a deacon; in the homily the mysteries of faith and the norms of Christian living are to be expounded from the sacred text throughout the course of the liturgical year.
>
> §2 Whenever a congregation is present a homily is to be given at all Sunday Masses and at Masses celebrated on holy days of obligation; it cannot be omitted without a serious reason.
>
> §3 If a sufficient number of people are present it is strongly recommended that a homily also be given at Masses celebrated during the week, especially during Advent or Lent or on the occasion of some feast day or time of mourning.
>
> §4 It is the duty of the pastor or the rector of a church to see to it that these prescriptions are conscientiously observed (Can. 767).

Paragraph 1 describes the essence of a homily and indicates the sources from which a homily should be developed. Coriden notes that the 1964 instruction[79] issued for the implementation of *Sacrosanctum concilium* gives a fuller description: "By a homily derived from the sacred text is understood an explanation either of some aspect of the readings from holy scripture or of another text from the Ordinary or Proper of the Mass of the day, taking into account the mystery which is being celebrated and the particular needs of the hearers."[80]

In speaking about the same paragraph (Can. 767 §1) Huels concludes that this norm is a constitutive law because the Pontifical Commission for the Authentic Interpretation of the Code of Canon Law states that a diocesan bishop is not permitted to dispense from the norm that reserves the homily to a priest or deacon. Explaining that constitutive law defines the essential legal elements of something, he summarizes what elements constitute a "homily": "According to Canon 767 §1, the homily contains four essential elements: 1) it is a form of preaching; 2) it is part of the liturgy itself; 3) it is reserved to a priest or deacon; and, 4) in the homily the mysteries of faith and the norms of Christian living are to be expounded from the sacred text throughout the course of the liturgical year."[81]

For Huels that third essential element of a homily implies that by definition a layperson cannot give a homily. "The legislator has defined the homily in a way that excludes its being preached by a lay person." But he is quick to add, "This does not mean that a lay person can never preach. Canon 766 says that a lay person can be permitted to preach. . . . When a lay person preaches, it cannot be called a 'homily' because that is impossible according to the way homily is defined in the law."[82]

Provost and Coriden concur with Huels in saying that the norm set up in 767 §1 regarding the homily is part of constitutive law. However, they both differ from Huels in terms of the occasions when this canon applies. Whereas Huels considers this canon as applying to all celebrations of liturgy, including all sacraments as well as the Liturgy of the Hours and even liturgies of the word, penance services, and other approved forms of worship, Provost and Coriden would limit the application of this canon only to the homily at Eucharist.

Huels contends that "if all four paragraphs of Canon 767 were referring only to the Eucharist, then this context should have been established in paragraph one." He further comments that if the legislator intended to limit this canon to a consideration of the Eucharist, then the legislator could have used the word "Eucharist" in 767 §1 instead of "liturgy."[83]

Referring to the same canon, Provost contends:

> While the description of the homily here is not exclusive to Eucharistic homilies, the context of the remaining sections of the canon argues for understanding homily here as applying only to those which take place during Mass. By law, a Eucharistic homily is reserved to a priest (in the sense of bishop or presbyter) and deacon. It does not seem that other liturgical homilies, outside Eucharistic celebrations and in liturgical rites which can be conducted by persons who are not ordained ministers, are necessarily included in the restrictions of this canon.[84]

Coriden, too, sees this canon as applying specifically to Eucharist: "The homily referred to in this canon (767) is that preached within the Eucharistic celebration. . . . This is clear from the context . . . from the sources . . . and from the explanation given by the Code Revision Commission."[85]

Despite their different interpretations of Canon 767 regarding the application of "homily" and "liturgy" in this canon, all three canonists, Coriden, Huels, and Provost, agree that laypersons can be authorized to preach at liturgy, even eucharistic liturgy, and that there is precedent for this not only in the early history of the Church but in the period following Vatican II.

Although Huels is convinced by his analysis of the law that a layperson cannot preach the *homily* at any liturgy, eucharistic or otherwise, he enumerates those cases in which the law specifically allows a layperson to *preach* at liturgy and indicates the documents that allow for that: (1) The 1973 Directory for Masses with Children "says that a pastor or rector of the church can permit an adult lay person to speak at a Mass for children after the gospel, especially if the priest finds it difficult to adapt himself to the mentality of the children"; (2) The 1988 Directory for Sunday Celebrations in the Absence of a Priest "allows the lay leader at a celebration of the liturgy of the word . . . to give an 'explanation of the readings' after the scriptures have been proclaimed"; (3) The 1984 *Book of Blessings,* 21, "allows . . . lay persons to be appointed to preside at various blessings, . . . [which] always include a liturgy of the word followed by an optional brief instruction on the readings, an exhortation or a homily."[86]

He comments that there is no reason the layperson could not give an exhortation or brief instruction, but that same layperson could not give a homily since that is restricted to a priest or deacon. Huels speaks of numerous other occasions when lay ministers could be authorized to preach; at the same time he acknowledges the difficulty of naming this preaching, since there is not yet "precise terminology" for such lay preaching.[87]

In his analysis of Canon 767 Coriden, too, speaks of the possibility of laypersons preaching at liturgy, even at Mass. Drawing on Canon 766, he comments that although the norm is to have the celebrant preach at Mass, or another priest or deacon if not the celebrant, "[t]his does not militate against various other forms of preaching by lay persons, when necessity requires it or usefulness urges it, even in the context of the eucharistic celebration."[88]

Examining the question of lay preaching at the Eucharist, Provost notes that the ordinary minister of preaching during Mass is the celebrant (presider), and in a liturgical sense, when another priest or deacon preaches in his place he is considered an extraordinary minister of preaching. He believes that although laypersons may not be permitted to preach a *homily* at Mass, there are occasions at which a layperson may be authorized to preach even at a Sunday Eucharist according to the norms of episcopal conferences, or in their absence, the ordinary of the diocese, or the pastor or rector of a church:

> On Sundays and days of obligation, a grave cause is required to omit the homily; if such a cause were to exist, as was admitted in the 1973 permission given the German bishops, it would seem a lay preaching could be delivered in place of a homily. The most common experiences of this have been when lay missionaries (for example, women religious working in foreign missions) are invited to replace the homily on a particular Sunday with an explanation of their work.[89]

Provost raises some interesting questions regarding the distinctions between a homily and other kinds of preaching. He asks: "What constitutes a 'homily' as homily and not some other form of preaching? Is it the content, i.e., the words that are said and the message they deliver? Is it the place in the celebration? Does it have something to do intrinsically with the individual who delivers it?" Noting that there are various opinions on this question, he says,

> The early distinction of the homily as based on the sacred text and adapted to the liturgical year is not substantially different from Canon 760's description of the ministry of the divine Word generally. There is nothing to impede other forms of preaching from having the same content, and even being delivered in the same style of preaching as a homily. For example, preaching during a retreat often bears these characteristics. Thus, it is difficult to see that the content necessarily differentiates a homily from some other form of preaching.[90]

In reference to Canon 767 §2, Coriden highlights the importance of the mandate to have a homily at Sunday Masses: "It is to be omitted only for a very serious reason. For example, if the celebrant is morally or physically unable to preach a homily, it would be preferable to have someone else preach it than to omit it." He notes, too, that paragraph §3 is a very strong recommendation for preaching at daily liturgies, especially at important seasons and liturgical events.[91]

In discussing paragraphs §2 and §3 of Canon 767, Provost makes a distinction between a homily being *required* at eucharistic celebrations on Sundays and holy days and being *encouraged* at weekday celebrations, and he comments that "even when it is required, a homily may be omitted if there is a grave reason."[92] In that case, a layperson may preach.

Summary

The above analysis of the revised code suggests a new *openness to lay preaching* in the Church today. In the spirit of Vatican II, the 1983 code explicitly calls the laity to the ministry of the word (cf. Canons 759 and 230 §3) and allows lay preaching in a church or oratory, which was not permitted in the code of 1917 (cf. Can. 766).

With reference to the issue of *preaching at eucharistic celebrations,* it is evident from the above discussion that the 1983 code leaves room for the possibility of lay preaching at Eucharist under certain conditions. The following summarizes the major points of that discussion: (1) A homily is required at Eucharist on Sundays and holy days of obligation; it is strongly encouraged at daily eucharistic celebrations and other liturgical events, especially during special liturgical seasons. (2) A homily at eucharistic celebrations by its very definition can only be preached by an ordained person. The ordinary minister of preaching at the Eucharist is the ordained celebrant (presider). Other ordained ministers who are not the celebrant are considered extraordinary ministers of preaching. (3) A lay person could be authorized to preach on Sundays or holy days if there were serious reasons for omitting the homily. If a layperson preaches at a eucharistic celebration, that preaching is not considered a homily but rather another kind of preaching. These serious reasons for which a layperson could be authorized to preach at Eucharist include: *(a)* in case of necessity, and *(b)* if it would be useful or advantageous. (4) A layperson could be authorized to preach at children's eucharistic liturgies (cf. Directory for Masses with Children). (5) A layperson could be authorized to preach at daily eucharistic celebrations since at these celebrations a homily is *strongly encouraged* but not required.

With regard to *preaching at liturgical celebrations that are non-eucharistic,* there is some disagreement among canonists about whether or not Canon 767 §1 applies to all of these liturgical celebrations or only to the Eucharist. However, there is general agreement among canonists that laypersons can be authorized to preach in a number of different circumstances. Huels cites some examples: (1) Sunday celebrations in the absence of a priest, (2) certain rituals of blessing in which preaching is a part, (3) liturgies of the word for catechumens, eucharistic exposition, funerals, non-sacramental penance services, celebrations of baptism, marriage, and so on.[93]

The above analysis illustrates that the 1983 Code of Canon Law leaves room for further expansion of the opportunities for lay preaching, even liturgical preaching. Effective implementation for broadening the possibilities for lay preaching will require continued dialogue in a spirit of discernment. To do this well it will be important to insure that various interpretations of the law be brought into dialogue with the historical data and the theological concerns discussed in the previous chapters of this volume. Perhaps the most important aspect of this dialogue is that it take seriously the experience of the People of God in the pews.

The last chapter will examine the present status of lay preaching in the Roman Catholic Church in the United States and will suggest a direction for the future.

4 Present Reality, Future Possibilities

In this chapter we will examine the growing practice of lay preaching as it is presently experienced in the United States. First, we will look at three examples of the practice of lay preaching in different parts of the country, which will serve as examples of the widespread and diverse practices that presently exist; next, we will look at the status of national and diocesan guidelines in the United States; finally, we will examine six fundamental questions that could serve as a basis for further reflection and discussion as we move into the future.

Lay Preaching Today

Lay preaching is alive and well in the Roman Catholic Church in the United States. In fact, it is an accepted practice in many parts of the country at the present time. Despite the minimal support it has received and the absence of consistent directives from diocese to diocese, it is a phenomenon with a real health and vibrancy that looks as if it will be with us for some time. To illustrate this, I will describe three concrete responses to the need for lay preaching in different parts of the country.

Northeast: Lay Preaching Formation

Recently a parish in the northeast invited me to facilitate a lay preaching workshop. The workshop was planned for anyone in the parish who was interested in learning more about lay preaching and preaching in general. Some who came were discerning the possibility of joining a lay preaching training program in the parish; others who were not considering doing any preaching themselves came to learn more about what was involved in preparing a homily or a reflection.

At the end of the workshop those who wanted to learn more about becoming lay preachers were asked to sign up for an interview with one of the pastoral staff members. Following the interviews, the staff, with each interviewee, mutually determined if the interviewee would participate in the training program for lay preachers scheduled to take place throughout the coming year. Some of the criteria for choosing a person for this ministry included active involvement in the parish community, a knowledge of Church teachings, theology, and Scripture, an understanding of liturgical ritual, and the ability to do public speaking.

The process of formation for lay preachers in this parish is focused on the Sunday Lectionary. Through study, prayer, discussion, and shared reflection those in training learn appropriate and creative ways to share the meaning of the Scriptures of the day in light of the particular liturgical season or feast and the experience of that particular community of faith. Lay preachers in training are expected to work with a staff member if they have never preached before.

This parish invites lay preachers to preach periodically at Sunday eucharistic liturgies throughout the year on those occasions when it is considered most advantageous to the parish community. The plan is to consider creating other opportunities for preaching in the parish as the process develops more fully. The process is still in place in this parish, and new lay preachers continue to be integrated into the parish ministry.

West: Parish Actively Seeking Women for Lay Preaching

Another situation in which I have experienced lay preaching is in a parish on the west coast. To ensure an active group of women lay preachers each year, staff members of this parish surface names of women who are active in the parish whom they think could become effective preachers in that parish context. The staff sends them a letter of invitation asking them to consider this ministry and to come to an initial explanatory meeting to discuss what this ministry entails. Because of the close location of theological schools in the area and the number of people who have had some ministerial experience and training, the staff has decided to invite to preach only those women who have completed their theological/pastoral studies or are presently engaged in them.

Discussion at the group meeting where the potential lay preachers gather for the first time centers on the nature of liturgical preaching, thus providing a common basis for further reading and reflection by the individuals. Some of the topics treated in this session include the appropriate use of Scripture for preaching with careful attention to understanding how to use certain passages in such a way that they do not foster anti-Semitism or portray any group of people in a negative light, discussion of the use of language and imagery to ensure inclusivity, the role of preaching in the context of Eucharist, and a discussion of the appropriate length of time for preaching. Each participant receives a copy of *Fulfilled in Your Hearing* to read and study during the year.

The parish gives these lay preachers approximately four opportunities throughout the year to preach at a Sunday eucharistic liturgy when it is considered most useful or advantageous to the parish. On that particular Sunday each one who has been appointed preaches at two Masses, giving her the experience of two assemblies whose approach to liturgical worship is somewhat different. In addition to the Sunday preaching, some of the lay preachers have the opportunity to preside and preach at Communion services, which are scheduled in the evenings twice a week.

There is no formal training program for these lay preachers other than the first meeting and some suggested reading. Since the women chosen to be lay preachers in the parish have been or are involved in a ministerial formation program that includes preaching preparation, the parish staff chooses not to set up their own program for training preachers at the present time. However, after each experience of Sunday preaching by the laywomen, the pastor writes each of them a letter in the name of the community to thank them for their service to the community and to give them some feedback from his experience of listening to their preaching. He makes a point of hearing each of them preach on the Sundays they are assigned.

In speaking about what he thought was needed to prepare lay preachers for preaching in the parish, the pastor said that since there are such rich resources in the theological schools in the area, he did not think it necessary to design a process in the parish itself. He acknowledged, however, that if, in another situation, resources were absent or limited, he would need to provide for that.

Midwest: Lay Parish Directors as Preachers

A few years ago I was invited to help facilitate a four-day preaching workshop for clergy in a diocese in the midwest. The bishop of this diocese had previously appointed a few laypersons to serve as parish directors.[94] Because of the shrinking number of clergy in that diocese at the time, the diocese was seeking to place at least three or four more laypersons in the same position. At present this diocese has almost tripled its number of parish directors.

During my work in the diocese, I learned that a major responsibility of these parish directors was to preside and preach at Sunday Communion services in the absence of a priest as well as at liturgies of the word, vigil services for the dead, and other worship situations. To be eligible for appointment as a parish director applicants, were required to be persons of integrity with a lived commitment to the teachings of the Church, have sufficient parish experience, a background in theology or religious education, and skills needed for the administration of the parish.

However, the diocese seemed less clear about what background and preparation were needed for the director's role as preacher. Although the parish directors had come into their new ministerial position with a good understanding of preaching and what it entailed, most had had little actual experience with preaching before they assumed this position. Many had received no formal training for preaching, since preparation for lay preaching was not a high priority for the diocese.[95] At that time the diocese had not yet determined what kind of ongoing training in preaching was necessary, although there was a strong commitment to continue choosing laypersons for this ministry. An occasional workshop and periodic meetings to discuss issues of common concern seem to be the primary modes of preparation for their preaching ministry, even today.

Though only a sampling, these three examples represent some of the diverse approaches to lay liturgical preaching formation and practice in different parts of the United States. They also illustrate what is not only a growing practice of lay preaching but a practice that is finding increased acceptability in the United States. It is apparent that in some places lay preaching is now an expectation of the worship community.

The Question of Guidelines

Despite this increased practice and acceptability, however, lay preaching is still a source of great confusion for many Roman

Catholics, particularly in trying to sort out the issues surrounding liturgical preaching. Thus we often hear such questions as: Is lay preaching really permitted; if so, when is it allowed? Why don't we have any lay preachers in our parish? Why can't women preach at Eucharist? When is the Church going to realize that many laypersons are well qualified to preach? Why can't laypersons preach at weddings and funerals? And so on.

It is understandable that there is still a great lack of clarity about lay liturgical preaching. Not only do the practices around the country differ greatly in some dioceses but they even contradict one another at times. In some dioceses, for example, it is understood that lay preaching is permitted in many different liturgical settings including Sunday eucharistic liturgies; in other places lay preaching is not permitted under any circumstances, despite the new position of the revised Code of Canon Law on the topic. In some dioceses the acceptable place for lay preaching at a Sunday eucharistic liturgy is after the Gospel; in others that practice is forbidden, and lay preaching may be done only after the postcommunion prayer. In one diocese the practice is to insert a reflection by a layperson at a Sunday eucharistic liturgy after the second reading but before the Gospel in order to avoid the impression that someone other than an ordained person is preaching a homily.

Some have suggested that the solution to this lack of clarity is to have national and diocesan guidelines (encouraged by the 1983 revised Code of Canon Law, 772 §1), which would assist and encourage local worshiping communities in implementing practices of lay preaching according to their specific needs and circumstances.

National Guidelines

Previously we noted that there are presently no approved national guidelines for lay preaching in the Church in the United States. Although the National Council of Catholic Bishops drafted "Guidelines on the Authorization of Preaching by Lay Persons in Churches and Oratories," which they approved at the bishops' meeting in November 1988,[96] the bishops were notified in a letter from the Congregation for the Clergy that the guidelines were not acceptable.[97]

According to Huels, the reason for the rejection was that the proposed "guidelines" would not have been binding, and the Holy See envisions such *praescripta* (Can. 766) as binding. "A prescript is a norm or rule, something that is prescribed, something that is required. A guideline is an optional directive. The intention of the NCCB was to issue guidelines and allow each bishop to establish a normative policy for his diocese on the basis of those guidelines. The Holy See found this unacceptable and refused to give its *recognitio*."[98] Huels notes in a later work that "[t]he NCCB's second attempt to adopt a policy on lay preaching failed to get the necessary two-thirds vote of conference members."[99]

Diocesan Guidelines

In September 1996 the Committee on Pastoral Practices of the NCCB sent a request to all dioceses in the United States for information about diocesan norms, policies, or guidelines concerning preaching by laypersons in churches or oratories. Of the fifteen dioceses from whom responses had been received at this writing, only five have any kind of guidelines, norms, or policy statements regarding lay preaching. Two other dioceses have established guidelines, but these had not been received by the NCCB office at the time of this writing. Thus we are aware of seven dioceses who have some type of guidelines for use in their dioceses.

Although the seven diocesan guidelines differ in style and detail, all agree on certain major points that reflect the directives of the 1983 revised Code of Canon Law: (1) the bishop of a diocese is responsible for overseeing preaching in the diocese; (2) laypersons are not permitted to preach a homily; (3) laypersons may preach at eucharistic liturgy on occasion when it is necessary or useful, but their preaching would not be considered a homily; (4) laypersons may preach at other specified liturgical celebrations when it is necessary or useful; and (5) laypersons must be suitably qualified to preach.

Two of the seven guidelines under consideration direct that the preaching by a layperson at a eucharistic liturgy should be done after the closing prayer and before the blessing and dismissal rather than after the Gospel. One mentioned other possible placements such as before the Liturgy of the Word or after a homily when that is required: practices that have been widely criticized because of their lack of attention to good liturgical principles.[100] One of these guidelines mentioned other places where remarks by laypersons would be appropriate: at the opening of Mass either before the entrance procession or right before the formal greeting by the presider.

The study of these diocesan directives for lay preaching from seven dioceses in the United States reveals that at least in some dioceses the practice of lay preaching, although exercised with caution and some hesitancy, is officially supported and valued for its potential contribution to the life of the Church.

In the absence of any consistent approach at the diocesan level, however, pastors responsible for overseeing worship in their local setting are often hesitant to implement the practice of lay preaching unless it is clear that the bishop of the diocese will not object. As a result, even at a time when lay preaching is permissible and encouraged by the spirit of Vatican II, the postconciliar documents, and the 1983 Code of Canon Law, it is frequently treated as a great exception to the rule, an aberration, or completely unauthorized. In many instances the question of liturgical preaching by laypersons is simply ignored; it is not considered by the majority of Roman Catholics to be either a possibility or of real value. In fact, lay preaching is one of the best kept secrets regarding lay participation in the Roman Catholic Church today.

There is some disagreement about the value of having national or diocesan guidelines for lay preaching. Some believe that guidelines would stifle the creative use of lay preaching currently in place at the local level and would prohibit a local church from deciding when lay preaching is necessary or useful in its own situation. Others believe that having guidelines in place would both encourage lay preaching to flourish and prevent a certain arbitrariness of decision making against the practice of lay preaching, especially in dioceses that do not officially recognize or value it.

Possibilities for the Future

As we witness the turning of the millennium, it seems timely to assess the practice of lay preaching in the present in order to consider how we can integrate the best insights of our tradition with the contemporary needs and experiences of God's people and thereby create new possibilities for the preaching and hearing of the word of God for the future Church.

In this volume we have tried to highlight the important historical moments pertaining to lay preaching, raise some of the more pressing theological and liturgical concerns for further investigation, and summarize the position of the 1983 Code of Canon Law regarding lay preaching. In addition, we have given examples of the actual practice of lay preaching in different parts of the country and discussed the present state of national and diocesan guidelines in the United States. We will now explore six of the more significant questions that need to be addressed in more depth in order to move the question of lay preaching to a new place. I hope in the pages that follow to pull out some of the significant threads that can be used in weaving a new garment of many textures, colors, and shades—the new garment of lay preaching—appropriate dress for the twenty-first century.[101]

Fundamental Questions

The first question and the one most commonly asked concerns the laity's mandate to preach. Some are asking if laity would have the mandate to preach if there were not a shortage of priests. In other words, are laity just filling the gap? It is not unusual to hear discussions about lay preaching beginning with the rationale that lay preaching is necessary because there are fewer clergy—not enough to meet the needs of God's people for hearing the word of God. Often this is the only rationale given. This question gets to the heart of the issue of vocation, or call. Are laypersons called to preach, or do they merely fill in when clergy are not available? Little attention is given to the call of each baptized Christian to preach the good news aside from whether or not there is a shortage; little mention is made of the value of lay preaching for enriching the expression of the preached word. Implied in these discussions is the unstated assumption that if there were enough clergy to preach laypersons would no longer be needed to preach.

Lynda Robitaille, among others, takes issue with that approach to the issue of lay preaching. She objects to those who suggest that if there were enough priests lay preaching would no longer be needed. In her mind the worst case scenario would be to let lay preachers help out temporarily until the Church has enough deacons and priests to fill that role. On the contrary, since laity are capable of preaching by right of their baptism and confirmation, the Church should rejoice in the recognition of the different roles they play because they are adult children of God. She notes that canon law, taking its direction from Vatican II, recognizes the capacity of laity to preach and to work in a cooperative way with bishops in the public ministry of the word of God.[102]

A second question that persists despite the many and detailed explanations given to resolve it is, What exactly is a homily? Whether we examine it from the perspective of theology or canon law, or from the perspective of the listening congregation, it is a puzzling issue. It is difficult to ascertain if a homily refers more to the content of what is preached, to the person who preaches it, or to the placement of the preaching in the context of the liturgy. Despite the many definitions and descriptions given in formal and less formal documents on the liturgy, the distinction between a homily and other forms of preaching is not that obvious.

Some question why a homily needs to be preached by an ordained person. If what is preached by a layperson and an ordained person has similar content, it is unclear why it matters whether the preacher is ordained or lay. It would seem that the important value is that what is preached truly leads the congregation to fuller participation in the liturgy. If what is preached by a layperson and an ordained person have basically the same content, why can't the preaching done by the layperson be considered a homily? To keep defining the homily as an act of the ordained does not appear to be satisfactory. People are struggling to understand the logic of this approach. Frequently the assembly experiences lay preaching as a powerful encounter with the word that leads them into deeper union with Christ. In their minds it is a homily, by whatever name it is called. And that, too, is problematic. It is difficult to know what to call the preaching done by a layperson in the context of liturgy if not a homily. No real name has been given to *what* is preached by a layperson.

The third question for our consideration relates to the issue of ministerial leadership in the eucharistic assembly and its relationship to preaching. This question looks at how the preaching role in the worship assembly can better reflect its communal and dialogic nature. Earlier, in chapter 2, we discussed John Baldovin's understanding of leadership of the Eucharist as a shared responsibility; he stated that "ministerial leadership of the Eucharist is not considered a solo activity." Baldovin calls for ministerial leadership to be a shared leadership and believes that a person's ability to share leadership is a desirable gift or quality of the ordained leader of the community.

It could be helpful for our reflection to apply this understanding of shared leadership to preaching as well as to the presiding role in the eucharistic liturgy. The homily is not an isolated act of the preacher, whether ordained or lay, but rather a dialogic act calling for the participation of both preacher and hearers in the preaching act. This approach underlines the participative nature of the homily and thus minimizes the emphasis on the one who preaches. Emphasizing the preaching role in the liturgy as one of shared leadership gives more significance to the gathered community's part in effecting the homily with the one who preaches. It also allows for the possibility of a diversity of preachers exercising the preaching role in the midst of the gathered assembly.

A questionable practice that is growing in many dioceses throughout the United States is the use of the same ordained preacher at several Masses on a Sunday, some at which he does not preside. This would require him and other priests to preach only once or twice a month, since they would be on rotation; in theory this would give each of them more time for preparation. Usually this priest is not present for the full Mass each time and is therefore not fully a part of each particular praying assembly except at that one liturgy at which he presides. This practice seems to sacrifice good liturgical principles for expediency and fails to acknowledge other viable alternatives for meeting the need for good quality Sunday preaching, such as trained lay preachers who would rotate regularly on the schedule with the ordained preachers. In addition, this practice of having a priest preach at several Masses on a Sunday in which he is not a participant for the whole eucharistic action raises many questions about the integrity of the eucharistic celebration, mentioned in chapter 2.

Some members of the assembly find it even more offensive when the priest-preacher is not a regular participating member of the community and has no real connection with them. They object to the use of what some have labeled a "rent-a-preacher" when members of their own worshiping community (lay preachers) could have preached instead.

The fourth fundamental question relates to "who" is preaching in our churches on a regular basis. Given the present reality of Roman Catholic clergy in the United States, they represent for the most part one segment of the population—white males who are not married. Therefore the majority of preachers do not represent either gender differences or the growing diversity of cultural and ethnic groups in our churches, making it more difficult for them to relate to the experience of those in the congregation.

Dolores Curran brings an urgency and poignancy to this question when she looks at the failure of the Church to include women in a significant way in the liturgical preaching ministry. She calls for taking some immediate action in inviting women to the pulpit, "because that is the only accredited voice in our church. It is the only place where ordinary laypeople consistently hear the Good News proclaimed." In her view, "[p]reaching is a meaningful role. It is where attitudes are changed, souls are awakened and the good news is made incarnate, which explains why recent church injunctions against women preaching are so strongly worded."[103]

Curran describes in some detail a number of reasons for needing women preachers, which reflect the views of other writers on this topic. She highlights her experience as a woman interested in marriage and family life issues, women's spirituality, and the overall contribution that women make to the world and the Church because of their different ways of experiencing the Gospels and the worlds in which they live. The concerns and strong feelings she expresses about these issues represent legions of women in the Church today whose patience is wearing and whose loyalty to a Church that fails to take them seriously is waning.

Similar concerns have been expressed by women from different cultural and ethnic groups who want to bring to the Church's attention the serious lack of attention to the needs of the listeners of diverse backgrounds in the present practice of preaching today.[104]

It could be helpful for our reflection to talk with women of other Christian churches who have been engaged in ordained and lay ministry, including the preaching ministry, for some time. They have struggled through the years with many of the same questions surrounding women's role in the Church, women's ordination, and women's right to preach. Although they have arrived at a resolution to some of these issues sooner than we, the tensions they experience are still very real, since the political, social, cultural, and ecclesiastical worlds remain steeped in old prejudices and mind-sets that are difficult to change, especially regarding women.[105]

The fifth fundamental question is the question of who has the authority to determine when and in what circumstances lay preaching may take place. As we look at canon law and the absence of national and, for the most part, diocesan guidelines, it becomes apparent to us that there is great ambiguity about this. Although there is no question that the ordinary of the diocese has responsibility for overseeing the ministry of the word in the diocese and that the pastor or rector can grant permission in the local setting, it is much less clear how this plays itself out in the concrete.

Canon law itself is somewhat ambiguous. The ordinary has the primary responsibility (Can. 756 §2) for the particular diocese entrusted to him, yet in Canon 767 §4 the pastor or rector has the responsibility to be sure that the provisions of that canon are carried out. What if they interpret the needs of the people differently?

Canon 766 mentions that laity may be permitted to preach in a church or oratory if it is "necessary" or "useful" in certain circumstances. But it is not clear who determines that. The wording of this canon implies a freedom of choice in determining those occasions that meet the criteria of necessity or usefulness and provides an opening for decision making at the local level, yet it is difficult to know who has the actual authority in particular circumstances—the pastor, the bishop, or the episcopal conference. In terms of authorization for preaching it is important, too, to consider where the experience of the local community enters into the decision-making process. It is essential that the local community would collaborate in the process of choosing the criteria for determining when lay preaching would be "necessary" or "useful." As we have noted above, there has been great confusion throughout the country because of the different approaches to resolving this question of authorization and for determining what situations meet the criteria of usefulness and necessity described by Canon 766.

This reflection on who authorizes lay preaching can lead us to look at the fundamental authority of the Holy Spirit. How do we as Church discern the Spirit's call to preach in those who sense that call and experience that call as confirmed by the community? If we limit our criteria for lay preaching to law alone, we are missing an important link with our tradition, which has honored since its inception the privileged role of the Spirit in leading and directing us, often to places where we would rather not go.

The sixth and last fundamental question that needs attention is the issue of formation for lay preaching. Formation or training for lay preaching is a topic that occurs quite often in conversation. Frequently expressed in terms of a fear or an objection, the comment is often made that just because lay preaching is possible does not mean that anyone who wants to should preach. The person who preaches must be qualified, must have the ability to do so, must have conviction, and so on. And just as frequently, someone will add that priests need the same criteria applied, too.

It is certainly true that not everyone has the ability to preach at worship. Although all of the baptized "preach" in the broad sense by the lives they live, something more than that is needed for liturgical preaching. But how do we determine what is expected of someone who does liturgical preaching?

Of the seven dioceses discussed above that have some type of norms, policies, or guidelines for lay preaching as of this writing, three listed qualifications or competencies or both needed by lay-persons in order to be accepted by that diocese to preach; the other four did not address this issue. One of these dioceses that listed both qualifications and competencies spoke of a training program that would assist them to achieve the stated competencies; another implied that potential lay preachers were to receive training at a specific place in the diocese. Neither elaborated on what that training would look like; however, the implication was that at the end of it they would be qualified preachers.

There were similarities in the two dioceses that listed their requirements in detail. Some of these included, for example, commitment to the Catholic faith; a sense of the community to which the lay preacher was going to preach; academic background in Scripture, liturgy, and related areas; communication skills; and cultural sensitivity and global awareness. One diocese made a point of mentioning that these qualifications were needed by all preachers in the diocese, not only lay preachers.

In our world of instant communication we are becoming more aware of the many ways in which "education" happens. We are educated, that is, we learn and are formed, in both informal and formal settings. We learn through logical discourse; we learn through our senses; we intuit meanings of poetry, literature, and symbols; we learn by participating in ritual—liturgical worship, the ritual of a football game—we learn by doing something such as baking a cake. Learning happens in many ways whenever we are open and in a posture of receptivity. And we even learn when we are not aware or too alert. At those times we learn by osmosis, so to speak. For example, we are just beginning to understand how much babies learn in the womb, and we are continually surprised at the long-term effects of learning in early childhood. We are discovering that learning is a complex phenomenon that permeates our entire lives.

Given this understanding of how people learn, it is difficult to judge preparation for preaching on the basis of certain "formal" requirements alone, since people are at such different starting points. In addition, some of the qualities needed for effective preaching are qualities of heart and spirit that cannot be easily evaluated.

For the more measurable competencies, perhaps moving in the direction of competency-based learning for preaching is the way to look at the issue of formation for lay preaching, as one diocese has done. What competencies are needed to preach well and effectively in the context of a community of faith?[106] Perhaps by reflecting together as local communities on what competencies are necessary for both *hearing* and *preaching* the word would be a way to begin to involve the local communities of faith in the process of formation of lay preachers.

Whatever approach is taken for the formation of lay preachers, it is essential to keep in mind that preaching at its core is an art—an interdisciplinary event that requires qualities of mind, heart, and spirit and that brought together in the act of preaching will invite the listeners to participate in the preaching moment as dialogue partners in the conversation.

Conclusion

In *The Shape of the Church to Come* Karl Rahner underscores the difficulty of the preaching task and urges preachers to exercise existential imagination so that they can preach to the "non-believers" among us, moving them to conversion and fuller freedom. Preachers need to maintain a realistic yet creative approach to their task, reflecting the struggle in which we are all engaged while at the same time offering hope in a world tempted to despair. God will redeem and liberate us only if we take the risk of preaching the message of God with strength and conviction. Rahner was convinced that "only when the message of the living God is preached in the churches with all the power of the Spirit will the impression disappear that the Church is merely an odd relic from the age of a society doomed to decline."[107]

As we noted in our introduction, the right and the need of the People of God to hear the word of God preached well and effectively is paramount. I believe that the word of God, "the message of the living God," can be preached effectively by both ordained and lay preachers, who share a common baptism and mandate for preaching. Together they can bring vitality and enthusiasm for the preaching ministry, which will feed the People of God in abundance, not unlike the miraculous event of the loaves and fishes—at first there was not enough to feed the people who were famished, and then there was such an abundance that there were baskets of leftovers that could be used to feed others.

And what is effective preaching of the word of God? The word of God is preached effectively when the assembly gathered, both preacher and listeners, become actively involved in the preaching act as participants; when the Word proclaimed and received interprets the lives and experience of the preacher and listeners in light of God's saving act in Christ. Preaching is effective when the gathered assembly is transformed—when they begin to see with new vision, hear with new acuity, and hope in new possibilities for themselves, the community, the world; when the word and works of justice, healing, and reconciliation are proclaimed unceasingly.

Notes

1. Term used by John W. O'Malley, "Introduction: Medieval Preaching," *De Ore Domini: Preacher and Word in the Middle Ages,* ed. Thomas L. Amos and others (Kalamazoo, Mich.: SMC XXVII Medieval Institute Publications, 1989) 2.

2. See J. Frank Henderson, "The Minister of Liturgical Preaching," *Worship* 56 (1982) 216; James H. Provost, "Lay Preaching and Canon Law in a Time of Transition," *Preaching and the Non-Ordained,* ed. Nadine Foley (Collegeville: The Liturgical Press, 1983) 139; John Burke and Thomas P. Doyle, *The Homilist's Guide to Scripture, Theology, and Canon Law* (New York: Pueblo Publishing Co., 1987) chapter 5; John M. Huels, "Lay Preaching at Liturgy," *More Disputed Questions in the Liturgy* (Chicago: Liturgy Training Publications, 1996) 189.

3. See James H. Provost, "Brought Together by the Word of the Living God," *Studia canonica* 23 (1989) 354–55.

4. For example, see Ruth Wallace, *They Call Her Pastor* (Albany, N.Y.: State University Press, 1992).

5. See the selected bibliography at the end of this book; also note one of the most recent treatments of this topic in Mary Catherine Hilkert, *Naming Grace* (New York: Continuum Press, 1997), especially chapters 9 and 10.

6. *Code of Canon Law: Latin-English Edition* (Washington, D.C.: Canon Law Society of America, 1983) Canon 759.

7. See Sandra Schneiders, "New Testament Foundations for Preaching by the Non-Ordained," *Preaching and the Non-Ordained,* 86.

8. O'Malley, "Introduction: Medieval Preaching," 1–2.

9. Ibid., 2.

10. Hilkert, *Naming Grace,* 144–48.

11. Ibid., 149.

12. Schneiders, "New Testament Foundations," 66.

13. Ibid., 68.

14. Ibid.

15. Hilkert, *Naming Grace,* 150.

16. *St. Leo the Great: Letters,* no. 119, trans. Edmund Hunt (New York: Fathers of the Church, Inc., 1957) 207–8.

17. James Coriden, "The Teaching Office of the Church," *The Code of Canon Law: A Text and Commentary,* ed. J. Coriden and others (NewYork and Mahwah: Paulist Press, 1985) 552.

18. William F. Skudlarek, "Assertion without Knowledge? The Lay Preaching Controversy of the High Middle Ages" (Ph.D. diss., Princeton University, 1979) 49–50.

19. See reference to *Statuta Ecclesiae antiqua* of the sixth century in Patrick F. Norris, "Lay Preaching and Canon Law: Who May Give a Homily?" *Studia canonica* 24 (1990) 444.

20. Thomas L. Amos, "Preaching and the Sermon in the Carolingian World," *De Ore Domini,* 41–52.

21. Yngve Brilioth, *A Brief History of Preaching,* trans. Karl E. Mattson (Philadelphia: Fortress Press, 1965) 69–76.

22. Kenan B. Osborne, *Ministry: Lay Ministry in the Roman Catholic Church* (New York and Mahwah: Paulist Press, 1993) 343.

23. Norris, "Lay Preaching and Canon Law," 445.

24. O'Malley, "Introduction: Medieval Preaching," 6.

25. Skudlarek, "Assertion Without Knowledge?" 54–59.

26. Hilkert, *Naming Grace,* 151.

27. Joseph R. Strayer, ed., *Dictionary of the Middle Ages* (New York: Charles Scribner's Sons, 1985) 5:191.

28. Norman P. Tanner, ed., *Decrees of the Ecumenical Councils* (Washington, D.C.: Georgetown University Press, 1990) 1:239–40.

29. Skudlarek, "Assertion Without Knowledge?" 360–64.

30. Norris, "Lay Preaching and Canon Law," 446.

31. Translations of the 1917 Code of Canon Law *(Codex juris canonici)* are taken from J. McVann, *The Canon Law on Sermon Preaching* (New York: Paulist Press, 1940).

32. Provost, "Brought Together by the Word of the Living God," 358.

33. Sacred Congregation for Divine Worship, *Directory for Masses with Children,* trans. International Committee on English in the Liturgy (1973).

34. Gary Macy, "The Eucharist and Popular Religiosity," *Proceedings of the Fifty-Second Annual Convention,* Catholic Theological Society of America (Minneapolis, June 5–8, 1997) 56.

35. Schneiders, "New Testament Foundations," 63.

36. Ibid., 64.

37. Decree on the Apostolate of the Laity, no. 3, *Vatican Council II: The Conciliar and Post Conciliar Documents,* ed. Austin Flannery (Collegeville: The Liturgical Press, 1992). All quotations from Vatican II documents are taken from this edition.

38. Dogmatic Constitution on Divine Revelation, no. 10.

39. Decree on the Church's Missionary Activity, no. 35.

40. Karl Rahner, *The Church and the Sacraments,* trans. W. J. O'Hara (New York: Herder & Herder, 1963) 18.

41. Patricia A. Parachini, "An Introductory Preaching Course within a post-Vatican II Theological Framework" (D. Min. project, The Catholic University of America, 1982) 41.

42. David N. Power, *Gifts That Differ: Lay Ministries Established and Unestablished* (New York: Pueblo Publishing Co., 1985) 52.

43. This issue will be discussed in more detail in chapter 3.

44. "The Role of Women in Evangelization," *Vatican Council II: More Post Conciliar Documents,* ed. Austin Flannery (Collegeville: The Liturgical Press, 1982) 319.

45. Mary Collins, "The Baptismal Roots of the Preaching Ministry," *Preaching and the Non-Ordained,* 114.

46. Ibid.

47. Ibid., 113.

48. Ibid., 113–14 (italics mine).

49. See Can. 767, no. 1.

50. Decree on the Ministry and Life of Priests *(Presbyterorum ordinis)* no. 4.

51. William Skudlarek, "Lay Preaching and the Liturgy," *Worship* 58 (1984) 505.

52. Ibid.

53. Ibid., 502.

54. J. Frank Henderson, "The Minister of Liturgical Preaching," *Worship* 56 (1982) 223–30.

55. Power, *Gifts That Differ,* 178–79.

56. Ibid., 178 (italics mine).

57. Collins, "Baptismal Roots," 129.

58. Ibid., 130.

59. Ibid.

60. John F. Baldovin, "The Eucharist and Ministerial Leadership," *Proceedings of the Fifty-Second Annual Convention,* Catholic Theological Society of America (Minneapolis: June 5–8, 1997) 73.

61. General Introduction to the Lectionary for Mass, no. 24, *Vatican Council II: More Post Conciliar Documents.*

62. *Fulfilled in Your Hearing: The Homily in the Sunday Assembly* (Washington, D.C.: United States Catholic Conference, 1982).

63. James A. Wallace, "Guidelines for Preaching by the Laity: Another Step Backward?" *America* 161 (September 16, 1989) 139.

64. Ibid., 139.

65. Ibid., 140.

66. Ibid., 141.

67. For example, see "Instruction on Certain Questions Regarding the Collaboration of the Non-Ordained Faithful in the Sacred Ministry of the Priest," *Origins* 27 (November 21, 1997) art. 3.

68. Provost, "Lay Preaching and Canon Law," 135. This was written before the promulgation of the 1983 revised Code of Canon Law.

69. All citations from the 1983 revised Code of Canon Law are taken from *Code of Canon Law: Latin-English Edition* (Washington, D.C.: Canon Law Society of America, 1983).

70. Coriden, "Teaching Office of the Church," 550.

71. Provost, "Brought Together by the Word of the Living God," 346–47.

72. Ibid., 351.

73. Coriden, "Teaching Office of the Church," 552.

74. Cf. note 3, above.

75. Provost, "Brought Together by the Word of the Living God," 356.

76. Ibid., 364.

77. Ibid., 357.

78. Huels, "Lay Preaching at Liturgy," 189.

79. See Instruction on the Proper Implementation of the Constitution on the Sacred Liturgy *(Inter oecumenici)* no. 54 (September 26, 1964).

80. Coriden, "Teaching Office of the Church," 553.

81. Ibid., 180.

82. Ibid., 180–81.

83. Huels, "Lay Preaching at Liturgy," 182.

84. Provost, "Brought Together by the Word of the Living God," 361.

85. Coriden, "Teaching Office of the Church," 553.

86. Huels, "Lay Preaching at Liturgy," 183–84.

87. Ibid.

88. Coriden, "Teaching Office of the Church," 553.

89. Provost, "Brought Together by the Word of the Living God," 364–65.

90. Ibid., 361.

91. Coriden, "Teaching Office of the Church," 553.

92. Provost, "Brought Together by the Word of the Living God," 363.

93. Huels, "Lay Preaching at Liturgy," 183–84.

94. See Canon 517 §2. Different terms are used in the literature to describe this position, for example, parochial administrators, supervisors of pastoral care, parish coordinators.

95. This was evident when we were invited to facilitate the preaching workshop for the clergy in the diocese. It was made clear that these parish directors were not welcome to participate in the full workshop with the clergy. Instead they were invited to participate in a half-day preaching practicum, which we facilitated for laypersons working in parish ministry.

96. See *Origins* 18 (1988–89) 402–4.

97. Letter dated February 12, 1990. See John M. Huels, "The Law on Lay Preaching: Interpretation and Implementation," *Proceedings of the Fifty-Second Annual Convention* (Washington, D.C.: CLSA, 1991) 61.

98. Ibid., 61–62.

99. Huels, *More Disputed Questions,* 192, note 1.

100. Ibid., 76.

101. Choice of this image influenced by Christine M. Smith, *Weaving the Sermon: Preaching in a Feminist Perspective* (Louisville: Westminster/John Knox Press, 1989).

102. Lynda Robitaille, "An Examination of Various Forms of Preaching: Toward an Understanding of the Homily and Canons 766–767," Address given at the Canon Law Society of America, St. Louis, Mo., October 9, 1996.

103. Dolores Curran, "Treading the Famine Road," *America* 173:17 (November 25, 1995) 9.

104. See Hilkert, *Naming Grace,* 175–81.

105. Ibid., 152–55.

106. See Parachini, "An Introductory Preaching Course," appendix B, 178–81, for a model of competencies needed for preaching.

107. Karl Rahner, *The Shape of the Church to Come,* trans. Edward Quinn (New York: The Seabury Press, 1974) 87.

Selected Bibliography

Amos, Thomas L., and others, eds. *De Ore Domini: Preacher and Word in the Middle Ages*. Kalamazoo, Mich.: SMC XXVII Medieval Institute Publications, 1989.

Aquinas Institute of Theology Faculty. *In the Company of Preachers*. Ed. R. Siegfried and E. Ruane. Collegeville: The Liturgical Press, 1993.

Baldovin, John F. "Eucharist and Ministerial Leadership." *Proceedings of the Fifty-Second Annual Convention*. The Catholic Theological Society of America. Minneapolis: June 5–8, 1997. 63–81.

Brilioth, Yngve. *A Brief History of Preaching*. Trans. Karl E. Mattson. Philadelphia: Fortress Press, 1965.

Burke, John, and Thomas P. Doyle. *The Homilist's Guide to Scripture, Theology, and Canon Law*. New York: Pueblo Publishing Co., 1987.

Canadian Conference of Catholic Bishops. "Decrees." *Studia canonica* 19 (1985) 174–77.

Carroll, Maureen, and Kathleen Cannon. "Enfleshing the Word: The Case for Lay Preachers." *Liturgy* 24:3 (1979) 31–34.

Castagna, Domingo. "Should the Laity Preach Today?" Concilium 33. *The Renewal of Preaching*. New York: Paulist Press, 1968. 92–98.

Castelli, Jim, and Joseph Gremillion. *The Emerging Parish: The Notre Dame Study of Catholic Life Since Vatican II*. San Francisco: Harper & Row, 1987.

Congar, Yves. *Lay People in the Church: A Study for a Theology of the Laity*. Trans. Donald Attwater. Westminster, Md.: Newman Press, 1959.

The Code of Canon Law: Latin-English Edition. Washington, D.C.: Canon Law Society of America, 1983.

Coriden, James. "The Teaching Office of the Church." *The Code of Canon Law: A Text and Commentary*. Ed. J. Coriden and others. New York and Mahwah: Paulist Press, 1985. 549–55.

Curran, Dolores. "Treading the Famine Road." *America* 173:17 (November 25, 1995) 8–11.

Documents on the Liturgy 1963–1979: Conciliar, Papal, and Curial Texts. Collegeville: The Liturgical Press, 1982.

Doohan, Leonard. *Laity's Mission in the Local Church*. San Francisco: Harper & Row, 1986.

_____. *Lay-Centered Church: Theology and Spirituality*. Minneapolis: Winston Press, 1984.

Flannery, Austin, ed. *Vatican Council II: The Conciliar and Post Conciliar Documents*. Collegeville: The Liturgical Press, 1992.

_____. *Vatican Council II: More Post Conciliar Documents*. Collegeville: The Liturgical Press, 1982.

Foley, Nadine, ed. *Preaching and the Non-Ordained: An Interdisciplinary Study*. Collegeville: The Liturgical Press, 1983.

Fulfilled in Your Hearing: The Homily in the Sunday Assembly. Washington, D.C.: United States Catholic Conference, 1982.

Gathered in Steadfast Faith: Statement on Sunday Worship in the Absence of a Priest. Washington, D.C.: United States Catholic Conference, 1991.

Grundmann, Herbert. *Religious Movements in the Middle Ages*. Trans. Steven Rowan. Notre Dame: University of Notre Dame Press, 1995.

"Guidelines for Lay Preaching." *Origins* 18 (1988) 402–4.

Hilkert, Mary Catherine. *Naming Grace*. New York: Continuum Press, 1997.

_____. "Women Preaching the Gospel." *Theology Digest* 33 (Winter 1986) 23–40.

_____. "Women and Priestly Ministry: The New Testament Evidence." *Catholic Biblical Quarterly* 41 (October 1979) 608–13.

Henderson, J. Frank. "The Minister of Liturgical Preaching." *Worship* 56 (1982) 214–30.

Huels, John M. *Disputed Questions in the Liturgy Today*. Chicago: Liturgy Training Publications, 1988.

_____. "The Law on Lay Preaching: Interpretation and Implementation." *Proceedings of the Fifty-Second Annual Convention*. Canon Law Society of America. Washington: CLSA, 1991. 61–79.

_____. *More Disputed Questions in the Liturgy*. Chicago: Liturgy Training Publications, 1996.

_____. "Sunday Liturgies Without a Priest." *Worship* 64 (1990) 451–60.

Hunter, David G., ed. *Preaching in the Patristic Age*. New York and Mahwah: Paulist Press, 1989.

"Instruction on Certain Questions Regarding the Collaboration of the Non-Ordained Faithful in the Sacred Ministry of the Priest." *Origins* 27 (November 21, 1997) 398–407.

Lathrop, Gordon W. *Holy Things: A Liturgical Theology*. Minneapolis: Fortress Press, 1993.

McVann, James. *The Canon Law on Sermon Preaching*. New York: Paulist Press, 1940.

Macy, Gary. "The Eucharist and Popular Religiosity." *Proceedings of the Fifty-Second Annual Convention*. The Catholic Theological Society of America. Minneapolis: June 5–8, 1997. 39–58.

Morrisey, F. G. "Decisions of Episcopal Conferences in Implementing the New Law." *Studia canonica* 20 (1986) 114–15.

Norris, Patrick. "Lay Preaching and Canon Law: Who May Give a Homily?" *Studia canonica* 24 (1990) 443–54.

O'Meara, Thomas F. *Theology of Ministry.* New York: Paulist Press, 1983.

Osborne, Kenan B. *Ministry: Lay Ministry in the Roman Catholic Church: Its History and Theology.* New York and Mahwah: Paulist Press, 1993.

Parachini, Patricia A. "An Introductory Preaching Course Within a Post-Vatican II Theological Framework." D. Min. project. The Catholic University of America, 1982.

Power, David N. *Gifts That Differ: Lay Ministries Established and Unestablished.* New York: Pueblo Publishing Co., 1985.

Provost, James H. "Brought Together by the Word of the Living God (Canons 762–772)." *Studia canonica* 23 (1989) 345–71.

Rahner, Karl. *The Shape of the Church to Come.* Trans. Edward Quinn. New York: The Seabury Press, 1974.

Robitaille, Lynda. "An Examination of Various Forms of Preaching: Toward an Understanding of the Homily and Canons 766–767." Address given at the annual meeting of the Canon Law Society of America. St. Louis, October 9, 1996.

St. Leo the Great: Letters. Trans. Edmund Hunt. New York: Fathers of the Church, Inc., 1957.

Schillebeeckx, Edward. *The Church with a Human Face.* New York: Crossroad, 1985.

Skudlarek, William F. "Assertion Without Knowledge? The Lay Preaching Controversy of the High Middle Ages." Ph.D. diss. Princeton University, 1979.

_____. "Lay Preaching and the Liturgy." *Worship* 58 (1984) 500–6.

_____. *The Word in Worship.* Ed. William D. Thompson. Abingdon Preachers Library. Nashville: Abingdon Press, 1981.

Smith, Christine. *Weaving the Sermon.* Louisville, Ky.: Westminster/John Knox Press, 1989.

Smith, Patricia. "Karl Rahner, Pastoral Theologian." Ph.D. diss. University of St. Michael's College, 1977.

Strayer, Joseph R. ed. *Dictionary of the Middle Ages.* Vol. 5. New York: Charles Scribner's Sons, 1985.

Tanner, Norman P., ed. *Decrees of the Ecumenical Councils.* Vols. 1 and 2. Washington, D.C.: Georgetown University Press, 1990.

Wallace, James A. "Guidelines for Preaching by the Laity: Another Step Backward?" *America* 161 (1989) 139–41.

Wallace, Ruth A. *They Call Her Pastor.* Albany, N.Y.: State University Press, 1992.

Zikmund, Barbara. "The Struggle for the Right to Preach." *Woman and Religion in America.* Vol. 1. Rosemary R. Reuther and Rosemary S. Keller, eds. San Francisco: Harper & Row, 1981, 193–241.